THE FINANCIAL VERSE

HARRY N. STOUT

The FinancialVerse - Guide to Savings

© 2020 by Harry N. Stout

ISBN: 978-1-09834-826-7 (print)
ISBN: 978-1-09834-827-4 (eBook)

TABLE OF CONTENTS

PLEASE READ BEFORE YOU PROCEED

or tax advice. As written in this book, the reader is encouraged to consult a licensed financial professional, tax advisor or attorney on these matters.

Thank you for purchasing this FinancialVerse book and investing in your financial literacy.

INTRODUCTION AND HOW TO USE THIS GUIDE

Would you like to save cash in these pandemic-filled days? Cash is more precious a commodity than it has been in years. Do you know where to look for discounts and value purchases? Are you too busy to research cash saving ideas? You have purchased the right book. We will help you answer these questions and many more. We have packaged the information in this cash savings guide to make your financial life a bit easier.

According to the Bureau of Labor Statistics (BLS) Expenditure Survey released on September 9, 2020, the average American household spent $63,036 in 2019. Do you think that households could reduce some of their spending? Could your family find ways to save money?

Let's delve a little deeper into these questions:

> How much do you think you could save of that $63,036?

> Could you save at least 1% or 2% or $630 to $1,260?

> Has COVID-19 reduced your spending? Forced you to save?

> Could the savings generated be used to help pay off debt? Add to your emergency fund? Add to your savings for your later years?

> Are there new ways to save money?

The answer to each of these questions should be a resounding yes. The next question you might ask is, Where should I start looking for savings? I believe you will be able to find at least 1% or $630 of savings from the ideas presented in this book. If it takes you three hours to read this book, that more than covers the book purchase price and compensates you at over $200 per hour for your time. Not a bad return on investment.

In *The FinancialVerse Guide to Savings – 600 Practical Cash Savings Ideas*, I will try to help. This guide was created to provide, in one place, a compendium of the cash savings ideas that have been presented in our MoneySavers posts, FinancialVerse books and from the author's experience saving money. All ideas presented have been written considering the pandemic and what it has done to our lifestyles. We have organized the ideas by major topic to make it easier for you to find ways to save cash and to make your world a better place. For example, if you are looking for ways to reduce your transportation costs, simply go to the Transportation section.

We hope you find this guide useful. If you have additional items you think we should include in our next update of this guide, just send them to us by completing the contact form on the FinancialVerse.com website. Have fun finding ways to save your precious cash.

Before we look at individual areas, here is how the average household spent their money according to the BLS 2019 Consumer Expenditure Survey.

Housing	$20,679	33%
Transportation	10,742	18%
Food	8,169	13%
Personal Insurance and Pensions	7,165	12%
Healthcare	5,193	8%
Entertainment	3,050	5%
Cash Charitable Contributions	1,995	3%

Other	1,891	3%
Apparel and Services	1,883	3%
Education	1,443	2%
Total	**$63,036**	**100%**

As you can see, housing, transportation, food, healthcare and the insurance categories make up approximately 76% of what households spent. I believe you can find numerous ways to save money and divert it to your savings and other needs.

CHAPTER 1

GETTING STARTED - YOUR JOURNEY TO SAVINGS

You just bought a new book on 600 ways to save cash. So where should you start? How do you factor in our pandemic-influenced world? Where do you begin your journey? I believe the best way to plot your actions is to take three simple steps:

1. Revisit your personal financial values

2. Set your savings goals

3. Agree on timeframes to meet your goals

THE IMPACT OF THE PANDEMIC ON SAVINGS

One of the frequent questions I am asked is, given the pandemic, should a household rethink their basic financial values and goals? I believe that now is a great time to do a money reset. Money is a much more precious resource for all of us than it was prior to the start of the pandemic. This is where what you spend and looking for cash savings comes into focus. You need to begin with the end in mind guided by your financial values.

WHAT ARE YOUR PERSONAL FINANCIAL VALUES?

Personal finance is different for everyone because it is just that—personal. The root cause of why there is so much variety in how people handle (or don't handle) their money is because we all have different matters that are important to us. What we value in life influences the kinds of goals we set for ourselves, and our individual goals will determine the actions we take to reach them. If you can understand what drives your decisions, you can better manage your financial affairs and get the cash savings you need.

Financial values are a person's or household's principles or standards of behavior when it comes to money. They are the judgments about the importance of money. It is a great exercise for you and your partner (if you are in a household) to take 30 minutes and talk about the key matters that you value most in life—what brings you the most joy, what you're striving to achieve and how you how you want to spend your non-work-related time. Make a list of them and, if possible, identify how money relates to supporting those values and making them happen. I will give some examples of how to do this later.

Financial values fundamentally boil down to agreeing on the purpose of money in your life. If you cannot agree on this, you won't know which savings ideas will work for you. Some examples of values are how much non-work-related free time you want, how large a family, how much travel you want to do, what charitable contributions you want to make, the importance of your self care and where you want to live—in the suburbs or in a large city. Answers to these value questions will each have a monetary impact on your spending decisions. Investing the time to agree on your money values will also minimize conflicts about how to manage money in your relationships. I have learned that if you can agree on the major values, the day-to-day minor issues take care of themselves.

SAMPLE QUESTIONS TO ASK YOURSELF ABOUT MONEY

Let's take a look at key money areas and the questions you should ask yourself as you develop or revisit your financial values.

Money Knowledge

1. What is the level of your money knowledge?

2. Have you taken a personal finance course?

3. What did your parents teach you about money?

4. How much time do you spend each week learning about money?

Lifestyle

1. What kind of lifestyle do you want?

2. Are you financially secure? If not, how badly do you want to be?

3. Do you want to travel and to where?

4. Do you need to keep up with your friends' lifestyles?

5. How much time do you want to devote to work? Do you live to work or work to live?

Earning

1. How do you feel about your current income? Are you making what you deserve?

2. How do you feel about your future earning potential?

3. Do you want or need a side gig?

4. Do you need to upgrade your skills to get a better job?

Spending

1. Do you consider yourself a spender?

2. How often are you an impulsive spender?

3. What is your biggest weakness when it comes to spending money?

4. What are your philosophies on spending?

5. Do you plan your big purchases?

Debt

1. How much debt do you currently have?

2. Are you current with all of your debt service payments?

3. Do you know and manage your credit scores?

4. If you want to buy something, are you opposed to going into debt to buy it?

5. What is your feeling about keeping a balance on your credit cards?

6. Do you want to live a debt-free lifestyle?

7. What are your overall thoughts about debt?

Saving Money

1. Which is more important to you, saving money or paying down debt?

2. Do you have an emergency fund? Do you think you need one?

3. Do you consider yourself a natural saver?

4. Do you have an ongoing effort to reduce your living expenses?

5. What are your thoughts about saving money?

Managing the Details

1. How much time do you spend each week managing your money?

2. How do you stay on top of your personal finances?

3. Are you financially organized?

4. Did you know that keeping track of finances is the foundation to personal finance success?

5. How do you keep track of your finances? Do you use a budget app?

The answers to these questions and other you will come up with should translate into money actions you should take to reach your goals. Here are some examples of financial values and how they translate into goals to act upon.

Financial Value	Sample Goal
Financial Security	Have a fully funded emergency fund
Travel Annually	Save $400 monthly for one big trip per year
More Family Time	Live on one income or be a part-time contract worker
Improve Health	Workout at home with your own equipment
Help Others	Give $200 cash to charities monthly

A key part of agreeing on your values and setting goals is to give each goal a timeframe for completion. For example, you will have a fully funded emergency fund within 9 months of your start date. I have learned that being as specific as possible with your values, goals and timeframes, leads to more success. As I think about this process, I always remember the saying—*If you don't know where you are going, you'll end up someplace else.*

SUMMARY

The pandemic has created the necessity for all of us to reconsider our approaches to money. Many of the rules of how to handle money have changed for the short and long term. You should sit down and objectively revisit your financial values, goals and targets in light of what has happened and what you have learned. Be sure to be honest with yourself and answer your own set of questions. It is always amazing to me that once the facts are known, people will take the right cash savings actions to address their situation.

CHAPTER 2

AREAS FOR SAVINGS

Below you will find the major topical areas that have been identified for you to look for savings. I have tried to present the major ideas I have personally used and where I have benefited.

BIG PURCHASES

1. **Always price check your big purchases.** In my view, these are purchases over $200. There are a number of apps that can facilitate the checking process. That way you can be sure to always get the best price. For example, Wikibuy is a great price check app that can save you money in a couple of different ways. Whenever you're looking to buy something online, Wikibuy will quickly search the web to make sure you're paying the lowest price possible. They'll also look to apply any coupon codes that have been successful for other Wikibuy users.

2. **Use the 30-day rule.** When you want to make a large purchase, think about it for a while first because, for some people, money is an emotional issue. Write down what the purchase is and how much it costs. If after 30 days you still feel it's necessary, purchase it. Carefully consider why you are buying before you take the leap to purchase.

3. **Never buy "off the shelf."** Any time you plan to buy something costly you should always do your homework first. Try the following: (1) surf the web to see who has the item at the lowest price, or if any sales are coming up, (2) check the website of the manufacturer and retailer to see if any coupons are available and (3) see if you can buy the same item second hand. By adding research to significant purchases you can save hundreds of dollars each year. For appliances and electronics, I always consult <u>Consumer Reports</u> to see if any key information about an item is available.

4. **Time major purchases for sale periods.** Because demand fluctuates by the season for certain items, you can time your big buys. For example, the end of model year or month-end can be a great time to buy a car because dealerships want to meet their sales quotas. January is a great time to purchase linens. Lastly, pay close attention to special deals on your favorite websites.

5. **Save for big purchases a little at a time**. Set up a fund that allows you to accumulate funds for your big purchases–these are called sinking funds. For example, these funds allow you to have the cash to replace those balding tires. Or you can save up for Christmas all year long since you know it's coming December 25. You do all of these things by setting aside money each month for that big purchase.

BUDGETING

6. **Create a budget.** Budgets help people manage their money better. It's that simple. Budgets are great and one of the best ways to save money because they keep you mindful of your cash income

and expenses. With a budget, you will know exactly how much you can spend in a category each month, how much you have to work with and what spending areas need to be evaluated, among other things. Budgets have helped people reach their goals, pay off debt, make more money, retire and more. This is one of the saving tips that will completely change your financial life.

7.   **Be aware of what you are already spending.** As you begin to look at your spending decisions, it is best to begin by taking a minute to look through your monthly expenses. You might be surprised how much you're spending. Being aware of your biggest bills is going to help when you're looking at the money saving tips.

8.   **Budget for regular maintenance of your vehicle, home and appliances.** When you're on a tight budget, it's easy to ignore long-term expenses like car repairs and appliance maintenance. It is much cheaper to pay for an annual tune-up of your HVAC system than to deal with major problems down the road. You might want to buy the maintenance plan for your car to minimize the potential cash outflow for repairs.

9.   **Set aside cash for irregular expenses**. Set up a monthly line item in your budget for bills that don't come due every month. One example is your ongoing medical bills. If you know that you will spend around $600 every year, put $50 a month in savings. So when the inevitable doctor's visit or prescription happens, you don't have to charge it on a credit card. In the meantime, draw interest rather than having to pay it to someone else because you didn't plan in advance. In my household, we spend about $6,000 annually on healthcare for medications, coinsurance and

deductibles. By budgeting this each month, I accumulate the cash needed to make the payments when they come due without incurring any interest costs.

10.   **If you live in a household, do the budget together with everyone contributing to paying the bills.** If you're married, sit down once a month and have family budget fun time. You need to get on the same page with money. Set goals together and plan how you will use your savings. Remember, it is your collective responsibility for the money in your household, not just one person's efforts.

11.   **Consider using a budgeting app.** You should have some type of budget in place. You may want to consider using an app like Mint that keeps track of your spending goals, expenses and budgets. This can be an easy way to see how you're doing and get more familiar with your finances.

12.   **Create clear money goals.** To achieve the best results, you need to have clear goals set about how you will live and what money means to your household. Goals give us a purpose and keep us motivated. If you need some inspiration, you can set financial goals like these: create an emergency fund, pay off debt, pay off student loans, purchase your first home or upgrade living arrangements.

13.   **Look to cut out items you will not miss.** Beyond finding ways to save money with your largest expenses, you can often reduce spending by eliminating any purchases or services you're not likely to miss. This can include cutting nice to have but unnecessary expenses such as subscriptions or video games. It's about

eliminating a series of expenses that can add up to a lot of savings.

14. **Cutting small or large amounts adds to savings.** As you better manage your expenses, you'll gradually direct your cash flow into your emergency fund or investments for the long-term. *For example,* if you cut an expense by $100 per month, that's $1,200 you can move into an income-generating investment account over the next year. Invested over 30 years in a mix of stocks and bonds averaging 7% per year, your $100 per month savings can grow to more than $117,000! That means saving just $3.33/day can equal a six-figure nest egg over 30 years.

15. **Let your kids know about the family budget.** Once your kids reach the 8-to-10 age range, you should consider involving them in the process of managing and saving money. It will help with developing good money habits. Some people share coupon savings with their kids. They do this for each coupon they bring home and split the savings with them. For instance, if they give you a fifty-cent savings coupon, give them twenty-five cents for their savings account. Thus, saving for both the family and the children.

16. **Plan next month's spending.** Budgeting apps like You Need A Budget can help you focus on where your money should go in the coming weeks, not just where it went last month. The online service offers a 34-day trial and claims to help new budgeters save an average of $600 in the first two months and $6,000 in the first full year of using the app.

17. **Prioritize cutting the biggest unnecessary expenses first.** You're probably familiar with the "80/20" rule. It holds that 80% of your

savings is going to come from 20% of your spending items. Cutting the biggest unnecessary expenses will produce the biggest savings. It is also easiest to eliminate those items you don't need and won't miss.

18.   **Set your spending and saving priorities.** What you value most is going to be where your money goes. After you have set up a basic budget, sit down and be sure the budget reflects the priorities for your finances. If getting out of debt is your main goal, make it a priority. If contributing to your emergency fund is the plan, make it the first target you hit before you move on to other savings goals.

19.   **Give every dollar a job.** To curb overspending, try to zero out your accounts. For one month spend the time to determine where each one of your hard-earned dollars went. This information will give you an awareness of your spending habits and will likely give you a road map of where to find unnecessary spending and future savings.

20.   **Celebrate hitting your budget goals.** Learning to have fun managing your money is always a good idea. So many people get tired of tracking outflows, paying off debt and saving money because it can feel so monotonous or they just lack the motivation. This is why I believe one of the best ways is to learn how to make budgeting money fun. This can help keep you motivated and interested in managing your money. My best suggestion here is to celebrate hitting or exceeding your budgeting targets by spending something on yourself. Give yourself some sort of positive reinforcement for a job well done.

CHILDCARE

....

21. **Consider cheaper childcare options.** If you are not working remotely, you should compare childcare options in your area to see if a cheaper alternative would be a better value. Or get creative by trying to cut back your existing childcare a day or two each week. Try working a later shift once a week so you can be home during the day. If you're lucky enough to live near grandparents, they might be willing to watch the kids part-time while you work.

22. **Reduce or eliminate organized child activities.** Activity overkill is something all parents have to confront at some time. The cost of your kids' activities can be really high if you don't keep it in check. To minimize these costs, look at the real expenses involved with any sport or activity before you let your children sign up. Meanwhile, keeping kids in a small number of focused activities can also help you save as much as possible and help keep you sane.

23. **Take your vacations during non-childcare time.** If your kids are having in-school classes, plan your vacation days on the days your children have half days of school or on teacher in-service days. It yields more time with kids and lower childcare costs.

24. **Create a babysitting co-op.** Check out local churches and community centers for babysitting co-ops or groups of parents that agree to help one another babysit at no cost. If there isn't one available in your area, create one. Also, there are sites to help connect families such as Babysitter Exchange.

25. **Use the benefit of a Flexible Spending Account.** Use a Flexible Spending or Dependent Care Account offered by your employer.

This account can be used to pay for dependent care services such as daycare, preschool and summer camps. You will be able to put pre-tax money from your paycheck into a dedicated account to help offset childcare expenses. The limit for contributing is $5,000 for a married couple in 2021. You save what would have been the income taxes on this amount as you contribute pre-tax dollars.

26. **Leverage your Child and Dependent Care Tax Credit.** If you can't contribute to a Dependent Care Account, take advantage of the childcare and dependent care tax credit.

27. **Ask local stay-at-home moms to sit for you.** Do you have a friend who is a stay-at-home mom that you trust? Sometimes these moms would love to care for an additional child in order to bring in a bit of extra cash. If your friend or neighbor doesn't run a licensed childcare facility, they'll likely charge lower rates. Just be sure to shop around for comparable providers so you can settle on a fair price.

28. **Look to hire an au pair.** This is an action that I took when my kids were older. Au pairs are often foreign young women (and sometimes young men) who want to live abroad for a period of time. You can often host an au pair as part of your family for a summer or even an entire year. Typically, this will cost less than a live-in nanny, but they do live with your family, which can be convenient if you're juggling hectic work schedules.

29. **Look to share the services of a nanny.** If you're more comfortable with the one-on-one care and flexibility a nanny offers, consider a nanny share. This is where you share a nanny with friends or neighbors located nearby. Nannies are often happy to do a

nanny share because it means higher weekly rates for them. Since you're splitting the rates with another family, you'll pay less.

30. **Plan ahead for summer childcare.** As your kids get older, having quality childcare during the summer months is especially important. To do this, you'll need to plan well ahead for summertime care for your school-aged children. The most affordable, high-quality options will certainly fill up first, so you'll want to get on that waitlist sooner rather than later.

31. **Find a parent's pandemic helper.** Parents who work from home usually find that they need some sort of childcare so they can actually get work done. One of the best ways to fill this gap is with a parent's helper. Since you're home working, you don't need an experienced high school or college student for this role. Often 5th and 6th-grade students from your neighborhood will charge an affordable hourly rate to entertain your kids while you're nearby in case of an emergency.

32. **Inquire about income-based options.** Some childcare centers, especially those run by non-profits, offer sliding-scale fees based on income. If you make too much money to qualify for state-based subsidies but not enough to comfortably cover childcare, look into daycare centers with these types of options.

33. **Fully understand and leverage your employer's maternity and paternity leave benefits.** More and more companies are offering longer maternity leaves, and even paternity leave. If your goal is to save on childcare, be sure you leverage these policies correctly, especially if you have two parents with parental leave benefits.

CLEANING

34. **Create your own cleaning rags and dust clothes.** Cut up old clothes that have holes or stains and use them around the house for cleaning, dusting and grease rags. You will buy less paper towels and other cleaning clothes.

35. **Make your razors last longer.** Save money on razors by drying the blades after each use and storing them in a dry space. This simple step can prolong the life of a razor blade by months. For more savings, consider switching to a service like Harry's that delivers inexpensive blades.

36. **Wash your own work clothing.** If you are still going to the office and need a lot of professional clothes for work, buy the generic equivalent of Woolite and wash your work clothing with it instead of regular harsh detergents. Initially, it costs a bit more for the detergent but saves your clothes from fading, thinning or frizzing, so you can wear them a lot longer and not have to buy new. Also, use Dryel instead of dry cleaning.

37. **Buy concentrate in bulk.** You'll save by buying concentrated cleaners that you dilute yourself—why pay for water? You are helping the environment and saving on shipping costs.

38. **Cut laundry detergents and clothing softener use in half.** Today, many laundry detergents and softeners on the market are highly concentrated. Be sure to use the smallest suggested amount. Our household has been doing this with softeners and it has really saved money.

39. **Only buy clothing that does not require dry cleaning.** This can save you time and money.

40. **Save on dry cleaning by carefully hand washing the item yourself.** When a clothing tag reads "dry-clean only," it doesn't necessarily mean that the item can't be hand-washed, especially if it's made of natural fibers. Garments that are simply constructed can sometimes be washed by hand or by using the delicate/hand wash setting on your washing machine. (Placing the clothing in a zippered laundry bag also helps reduce wear.) However, let your neighborhood dry cleaner handle anything with bright prints or colors that may bleed, clothing made of traditional silk or anything with delicate finishes.

41. **Save money by making your own cleaning solution.** A one-to-one mixture of vinegar and water makes an effective, economical multi-purpose cleaner. The non-toxic mixture disinfects floors and bathrooms and cleans glass without leaving streaks. Rest assured, its distinctive odor disappears as soon as the liquid dries.

42. **Use microfiber products.** These towels, mops and dusters are washable and reusable. They are designed to trap dust, liquids, oils and bacteria. For all of your new pandemic cleaning chores you can save dollars.

43. **Wash your laundry in cold water.** Unless you are laundering cloth diapers, there is very little need for you to wash your high-priced clothing in hot water. Turn the dial to cold, and you'll lengthen the use of your clothing and reduce your energy bill.

CLOTHING

44. **Swap clothes with a like-sized friend.** Before you buy a new out-fit, get some friends together and swap old pieces you don't want anymore. I have seen this work really well with the exchange of kids clothing and toys between neighbors and family members.

45. **Don't buy cheap clothes just to save money.** There are times when it makes the most sense to prioritize quality over price when purchasing clothes. An inexpensive shirt or coat is a poor bargain for older family members if it wears out in less than a year, but it could make sense for quickly growing children.

46. **Follow the rule of 30 times.** Many people say they won't buy a piece of clothing unless they plan to wear it at least 30 times and it matches other items in their wardrobe. This practice makes each piece of additional clothing something that is used and not just kept in the closet.

47. **Make your clothes last longer.** Your clothes will last longer if you give them a little bit of attention before you throw them in the laundry. It is best to prepare your clothing for the washer by closing zippers, fastening buttons and turning items inside out. Wash darks together using the cold-water cycle so they don't bleed onto light-colored clothing. If you have the luxury of hang-ing items to dry, it can help maintain their original size and appearance.

48. **Rent your formal wear.** If you have a one-time need for an ele-gant outfit, use a rental service like Rent the Runway or the Black Tux to borrow high-end designer items to keep you from spend-ing big bucks.

49.   **Spend only what you use on clothing.** We all have friends who spend a significant amount of money on clothes each month. The expenditure is their choice. That person can save money by buying fewer but higher-quality pieces and fully utilizing the wardrobe they already own. This practice can be learned and will result in large savings over a number of years.

50.   **Buy store brands instead of name brands.** You can find store brands that offer quality for a reduced price. It just takes some time to look for these items.

51.   **Learn how to dress minimally.** Buy clothes that mix and match well, and you won't need as many clothes. If you have seven pairs of pants and ten shirts that all go together, you can mix and match combinations that will look appropriate wherever you go.

52.   **Read care instructions on special garments.** Before putting that new shirt in the laundry, read the care instructions. You don't want to ruin a silk shirt or wash something that should be dry cleaned. Keeping your clothes in good shape will save you money and you won't have to shop as frequently.

53.   **Repair your clothing instead of tossing it in the trash.** My advice is to find a reasonably priced tailor or alteration shop in your neighborhood. It is better to make minor repairs to your clothing instead of paying to replace items. Don't toss out a shirt because of a missing button—sew on a new one or have it done for you. Don't toss out a pair of pants because of a hole in them— have them patched and save them for times when you're working around the house.

54.   **Shop outlet stores.** If you are looking for basic clothing and athletic wear, consider shopping at your local outlets. While the merchandise may not be of similar quality to retail stores, you can get reasonable, quality items for a good price. In some cases, you can get this year's fashions for way less. I have found the Tanger Factory Outlet Stores to be of great quality and variety.

55.   **Sort your clothes to maximize use.** Organize your clothes by category (i.e., pants, shirts, dresses, etc.) and color so you know exactly what you have. That way, when you need a particular piece of clothing you can find it and won't rush out to buy a duplicate.

COLLEGE FUNDING

56.   **Start planning for college early.** It is really important to have family conversations about college costs and how to pay for them. This includes clearly agreeing on the impact of the cost of the education on the future spending, retirement, savings and cash flow of the family and the student.

57.   **Start saving for college early.** If you know you're going to pay for some portion of your dependent's college costs down the road, some people recommend creating an account specifically for this expense as soon as the child is born. There are even accounts specifically designed to provide tax benefits to save for education expenses.

58.   **Make sure your student has skin in the college funding game.** Require that the student be responsible for funding a portion of the cost of classes and/or other related expenses with their own

cash. This experience will remind them to think twice about what they are spending. It will help avoid payment for unnecessary courses and educational expenses.

59. **Attend a lower-cost local community college for the first two years then transfer to a major institution to complete the degree.** Have the student attend a local community college or university system within the state where they are a resident to take advantage of lower in-state tuition rather than attending a costlier private or out-of-state public institution.

60. **Have your student take a gap year to mature, especially during a time when many colleges have moved to remote classes.** For many students it pays to take a year off after high school graduation for what is called a "gap year" to either work or travel to find out what they really want to do. By doing this, the student will be able to enroll in a college program firmly understanding the field they want to study with an additional year of maturity. This may help avoid the high cost of changing study majors.

61. **Understand what perks come with federally guaranteed student loans.** These loans come with some perks that may not be offered by private lenders, including income-driven repayment options, loan forgiveness programs and fixed interest rates. Plus, some federal loans are subsidized, which means the government will foot the bill for the interest on the loan while the student is in school.

62. **Understand the terms of private student loans.** Private loans come from banks, credit unions or schools. In some cases, nonprofit agencies provide a guarantee for student loans or lenders

may self-insure. A private loan may have a variable interest rate, which means the interest rate charged on the loan can change.

63. **Live off campus after your first year.** Living on campus can be expensive. You'll most likely end up paying far less for your housing and meals by living off campus. You'll need to do the research in your area to see if this applies to you as well, but it most likely does.

64. **See if you can pay for your dorm monthly.** Most colleges bill for room and board on a semi-annual basis. Investigate whether the school offers monthly billing. You may find you can save money on housing rates. If you have an income that would allow you to pay monthly and you don't have the cash to pay up front, this option could save you from having to take out a loan (and paying interest later).

65. **Continue applying for scholarships throughout college.** You may find you now qualify for scholarship funds based on how well you are doing or that new sources of scholarship money has become available.

66. **Plan to be done in less than four years.** I completed my undergraduate degree in a little over three years. If you're finding that college is going to be a financial burden, this might be an option to look into. Some of the tactics you can use to get through your program include taking far more credits than normal per semester (possibly 20 or more) or testing out of courses. This allows you graduate sooner but requires you to give up other activities.

67. **Take college classes in high school.** Some students take a number of classes yielding college credit—validate to make sure this

will happen—during their senior year in high school rather than opting for a free period or study hall on their class schedule. Have the student work with their guidance counselor to plan this. It can save money on the cost of a number of intro-level college classes.

68. **Get your textbooks for the lowest price possible.** Work to identify the books the student will need and investigate buying used books, library-available copies and lower-priced eBooks, if available.

69. **Get a part-time job or side hustle.** My freshman year, before I even started classes, I got a 20-hour/week job on campus working in the admissions office. Having a job during college helps offset educational expenses, provides work experience and also teaches maturity. If you are lucky, you may find a position in your field of study.

70. **Create a detailed education budget and manage it diligently.** Use all of the good money habits—track your spending, only use cash, buy second-hand technology devices, negotiate your bills and keep your credit in order.

71. **Use your imagination for cheap dates.** As you study, you'll need a social life. Look to keep your entertainment expenses to a minimum by taking advantage of free college lectures, exhibitions and sporting events.

72. **Use all of the resources in your college or university library.** Learn all that your library offers from books to video and special events.

73. **Learn some travel hacks.** Students like to travel. Learn to take advantage of college-supported programs, semesters abroad,

student travel discounts and ride sharing to get home for the holidays and special occasions.

74. **Track your educational expenses and deduct them from your taxable income.** If you are paying your own way through school, take advantage of educational tax deductions for tuition and fees along with tax credits given to students.

COUPONS AND DISCOUNT PLATFORMS

75. **Get free samples.** You can get free samples sent to you by websites Influenster and BzzAgent. All you need to do is write short reviews or tell friends about the products.

76. **Always ask for fees to be waived.** Any time you sign up for a service of any kind and there are sign-up fees, ask for them to be waived. Sometimes (but not always) they will be, and you save money just by being forthright about not wanting to pay excessive fees. If the fees are not waived, you may find you can avoid them by signing up for autopay or another billing arrangement.

77. **Ask about senior discounts.** Look for discounts at movies, museums, entertainment parks as well as restaurants, grocery stores and clothing retailers. My local grocery store has an age 65 and older discount day each Wednesday.

78. **Become a mystery shopper or reviewer.** You can save money on services, meals and experiences in exchange for completing honest feedback to companies. This can be especially effective if you use it to do things you'd normally do.

79. **Combine coupons with local sales prices.** Save coupons and use them in conjunction with sales at local markets. You can end up with items either being free or at a greatly discounted price.

80. **Follow "garage sale" Facebook groups.** People often pay full price for items they later realize they do not need or like and turn around and sell them. If you have children, you know how quickly they grow out of expensive retail-priced clothing. To help dramatically reduce this expenditure, look through local Facebook groups to see what types of gently used items are being sold by your neighbors. Join any garage sale groups that are in your area and browse through the listings throughout the day. It is easy to find groups that specialize in selling and swapping specific items that you may need.

81. **Don't forget the advertised price match guarantee.** Some major retailers, including Walmart, Target, Staples, Best Buy and Office Depot, now price match Amazon. There are many exclusions to watch out for but checking prices with a smartphone before making an in-store impulse buy can yield savings.

82. **For online purchases, check out Rakuten (formerly Ebates) as a source for discounts.** You can save money on your purchases and make money by inviting others to join.

83. **Get savings through social media.** Use social media, Twitter, Facebook, email, etc. and follow, like or subscribe to companies whose products you regularly purchase. You'll get all sorts of deals and offers that way. You might be better off using a different email account or setting up good filtering so you don't get overwhelmed.

84.   **Search online for discounts or promotional codes before you buy.** When you get to the shopping cart, you'll see a space to enter a coupon code or promo code. Instead of just making the purchase, do a quick search for your item plus "promo code."

85.   **Join American Association of Retired Persons (AARP) for discounts.** If you are over age 50, you can join and your annual membership is less than $20 per year. AARP offers its members a variety of valuable discounts. These include rental car, hotels, travel excursions and more. In addition, an AARP membership comes with many other benefits including savings on a Medjet membership; discounts at major restaurant chains, including Carrabba's Italian Grill, Outback Steakhouse and Bonefish Grill; and even save money on cell phone plans, home security plans and Audible memberships.

86.   **Pass on buying extended warranties.** A $49 two-year warranty extension on a $300 product may just not be worth it. Warranties are insurance, and we rarely need to insure something worth such a small amount.

87.   **Purchase discounted gift cards.** Websites like Cardpool and Raise allow users to sell gift cards they'll never use for a slightly lower amount than their full value. Consider buying gift cards to places you frequently shop to save instantly on everything you buy there.

88.   **Seek out free or low-cost membership cards.** Use a member card from your grocery store of choice. For example Publix, Target and Lowe's offer discounts if you use their credit card. Walgreens, CVS and other stores offer discounts and deals when

you use a member card at the checkout and many stores offer a club card or membership card.

89. **Request and follow up on rebates offered as incentives to purchase products.** After you buy a product with a rebate, send in the rebate form that day—don't hesitate. If you can, submit the rebate online for easier processing. Then set a reminder on your calendar to follow up with the company if you haven't received the rebate in a reasonable amount of time.

90. **Set up a sharing network.** Set up an arrangement with family, friends and neighbors to share power washers, lawn tools, lawnmowers and luggage. Within your family, look for ongoing savings by sharing phone plans or streaming video subscriptions. You'll need to agree on passwords and other logistical details, but they may be worth your while.

91. **Sign up for free loyalty cards.** Certain retail stores offer loyalty cards that make you eligible for additional savings. If you've skipped the loyalty card in the past because you don't want extra cards in your wallet (or on your keychain), you need to use the new apps. Apps like Keyring make it possible for you to always carry your loyalty cards without having to keep track of yet another card.

92. **Use cashback apps when you shop.** Here are two apps that allow you to save money on everyday purchases without having to jump through hoops. The first is Rakuten, which automatically tells you if an individual website is eligible for cashback. Rakuten is fully automated and is worth it to run in the background and save money. The second is Honey. Honey is a website you use to obtain promo codes or coupons to use when shopping online.

93.   **Use coupons from all sources.** You can find coupons everywhere these days and not just in newspapers or local magazines, coupons are available on company websites, apps like SnipSnap and online. Before you go out shopping, check your phone or computer and increase your savings.

94.   **Ask about student discounts.** Some clothing stores, including Madewell, Asos and Topshop, offer student discounts. Restaurants, grocery stores, movie theaters, gyms and technology companies also offer student discounts.

95.   **Look out for birthday freebies.** You may be able to find free birthday stuff by simply showing your birth date on your driver's license or by signing up for a company's email club to receive a coupon for your birthday.

96.   **Buy an Amazon Prime Membership.** I have found a Prime membership to be worth the money you'll save. Some of the things you'll get are free two-day shipping (and free same-day delivery if it's available in your area), access to streaming of thousands of TV shows and movies, unlimited photo storage and unlimited access to over one thousand eBooks, audiobooks and magazines.

97.   **Buy with reward points.** Don't spend more than you normally would but use a rewards credit card throughout the year and accumulate reward points for your spending. Then use the rewards for your Christmas gifts or to help with a vacation. The only caveat on this idea is to make sure you are not exchanging your points for much lower values than they are worth.

98. **Consider signing up for cash-back offers.** Take advantage of the fact that some major credit cards offer cash back on purchases. Sign your card up for these offers on the credit card website. Cash back is available from retailers as diverse as Amazon, Rite Aid and even Walmart and Kohl's.

99. **Don't forget to get Veterans' discounts.** Veterans can take advantage of a significant number of discounts and benefits. Marriott hotels offer military rates and Lowe's, the home improvement store, offers discounts to active and retired military.

100. **Get free makeup to offset your cosmetics budget.** Consumers looking to score free samples of face creams, toners, mascara and other everyday cosmetics and essentials should check Nordstrom, Belk and other upscale retailers for classes and events.

101. **Get paid for shipping with Amazon Prime.** If you have Amazon Prime (meaning you often get two-day shipping for free), you can opt for slower shipping on some orders to get other discounts, like $1 off Kindle books or Amazon music or money toward a Prime Pantry box.

102. **Get store refunds.** Paribus is a free service that can save you money on your online purchases even after you shop! Paribus gets you money back after you buy something and it goes on sale. You are guaranteed the difference and this service promotes that you get the money effortlessly!

103. **Maximize bargains from yard sales.** Yard sales are a great place to score awesome deals on items you need anyway—think lawn

tools, housewares, shoes or even sports equipment. The key is you have to be careful not to use the low prices found at sales as an excuse to buy things you don't need. At the next garage sale, limit yourself to items that were already on your list of things to buy.

104. Order free samples online.

105. Save money with apps. Use mobile apps to help save money while shopping for groceries, clothing and everything else. Try the RetailMeNot, Ibotta, Checkout 51, GrocerySmarts and SmartSource apps.

106. Shop at warehouse clubs without a membership. You can buy prescription drugs or alcohol at Costco or Sam's Club without being a member.

107. Sign up for every free customer rewards program you can. No matter where you live, you'll find plenty of retailers who are willing to reward you for shopping at their store. In order to protect your personal information create a separate email address just for these mailings, collect every card you can and then check that account for extra coupons whenever you are ready to shop.

108. Sign up for Swagbucks and InboxDollars. Swagbucks allows you to earn Amazon gift cards with very little work. Swagbucks is just like using Google to do your online searches, except you are rewarded points for the things you do through their website. Then, when you have enough points, you can redeem them for cash, gift cards and more. Another such site is InboxDollars. Here you can earn cash by taking surveys, watching videos, playing games, shopping online, redeeming grocery coupons and more.

109. **Track price drops.** Savings need not stop after you make that purchase. Several web-based services alert shoppers to after-the-fact price drops so shoppers can ask for a refund of the difference—or get one automatically (minus a cut for the service). Paribus and Rakuten monitor select retailers, including Amazon, through users' email accounts. Several credit cards offer a similar service for free.

110. **Try name-your-price sites.** Priceline, Hotwire and other travel sites aren't the only ones that let consumers name the price they want to pay. Greentoe has a similar setup for photography equipment, home theater items, appliances and more.

111. **Use a grocery couponing app.** Instead of printing and clipping coupons, use an app that is store specific or use one of the general apps such as SnipSnap, Shopkick or Yowza. This practice gives you the benefits of coupons without all of the time to organize them.

112. **Use deal-of-the-day sites such as Groupon.com.** This is a fantastic site to get some great group deals from local businesses. The only thing to watch out for is to buy only what you need and not what is offered simply because you can get a bargain.

113. **Use free shipping codes.** Look for free shipping codes or free shipping altogether. You can check out RetailMeNot. You can also sign up for a free Amazon Prime trial and get free shipping—just make sure you cancel after the trial if you are no longer interested in Prime.

114. **You can earn Starbucks rewards at home.** You can receive Starbucks stars, redeemable for free drinks and treats at the coffee

chain's stores, when you purchase certain Starbucks products at the supermarket. Enter your stars via the app or website by using the code on the package or upload a receipt for proof of purchase.

CREDIT CARDS

115. **Apply for a cash-back credit card.** As we all know, it's easier to overspend with cards—but they can be used responsibly too. Go to Creditcards.com to research cash-back cards that are best for you.

116. **Get a card that rewards points that you can exchange for travel or merchandise.** Many of these cards don't have an annual fee. With my rewards cards I manage to pay for at least two weeks of hotel stays per year. Go to Creditcards.com or The Points Guy to get more information on this idea.

117. **Sign up for credit card balance and payment due date alerts.** Get in the habit of paying on time and staying well below your card's maximum limit. Credit card balance alerts can also help you manage your credit utilization and keep you aware of how you may be overspending.

118. **Limit your credit cards.** Not using more than a certain percentage of your credit limit is a great practice that takes discipline. Cutting down on the amount of credit you use relative to your credit card limits is a great way to improve your credit management and credit scores.

119. **Look to negotiate rates with your credit card company.** If you're paying a lot of interest on your credit cards, it's important to know that you do have some power as long as you've been making your payments. You have the right to negotiate your current interest rate with your credit card issuer. Start by calling your card issuer at the number on the back of your card and explaining your request. If this fails, remember you can look to transfer your balance to another company that allows transfers and you may save money in the process.

120. **Get hotel or airline rewards for every dollar you spend.** Even infrequent travelers can save money by enrolling in airline and hotel loyalty programs. For example, basic hotel membership usually comes with free WiFi, late checkout and complimentary newspapers at some chains. Airline rewards cards will also allow you to check bags for no fee.

121. **If your credit score is good enough, look to transfer your high interest credit card balances to 0% APR cards.** Since the onset of the pandemic, many issuers have placed restrictions on transfers so there are less such offers available.

122. **Make a credit payment each week.** It will help you reduce interest costs, stay on top of what you have been spending and will also keep your credit utilization lower throughout the month. It is a way to develop the habit of paying off your credit cards in full each month.

123. **Pay off credit cards in full each month.** Although cash back and rewards cards can provide you with great value, the cash and miles are only valuable if you're not falling into debt or paying interest to qualify for them.

124. **Shop with cash or debit cards, not with credit cards.** To keep you focused on reducing your high interest rate credit cards, only shop with cash and debit cards. With cash and debit cards you're paying based on what currency you have in your pocket and there's no chance of getting into debt. That reality will also prevent the possibility of spending more money than you have.

125. **Take advantage of your credit card's added benefits.** Did you know that, in many cases, if you buy plane tickets with your credit card, you get automatic travel insurance? Many people don't know this and end up buying a separate insurance policy—which is money that could be spent on your actual holiday! Other cards provide free extended warranties on items that you purchase with them or insurance for rental cars that are paid for with the card. Take the time to understand the added benefits each of your credit cards offer.

126. **Use a credit card debt calculator.** Even if you think you're paying off your credit cards on time, you may not be paying them off as aggressively as you should to save yourself from those high rates of interest. That is why a credit card debt calculator—such as CreditKarma's—can come in handy. The calculator will allow you to see what kind of monthly payments you would have to make— and for how long—in order to become debt free.

CREDIT SCORES

127. **Focus on cleaning up your credit card record.** The most important factor that affects your credit score is your credit history. Your credit score, in turn, can determine what interest rates you get on

auto loans, credit cards and more. Look to see that you do not have any negative remarks or errors on your credit record. Get copies of your credit reports and dispute any issues by directly contacting the credit bureaus, such as Transunion or Equifax. Monitor your scores regularly and, if you see any errors, dispute them right away to make sure you aren't getting locked into higher rates due to mistakes or inaccuracies.

128. **Your credit score directly translates into a rating level that institutions use to grant you credit at reasonable terms.** Using the FICO credit score scale, which ranges between 300 on the low end to 850 on the high end, the categories are as follows based on your score: Very Poor 300-579, Fair 580-669, Good 670-739, Very Good 740-799 and Exceptional 800-850. Know your score and what category you are in and you can save money on your borrowings and other products.

129. **Don't pay for your credit report.** Instead, visit AnnualCreditReport.com and get your truly free credit report. Get your credit score from the source at MyFICO.com. Also, take advantage of credit sites such as freecreditreport.com or freecreditscoreonline.com.

130. **Once your credit report clean-up is done, check your credit report for free once a year.** Use your annual free credit report from the three credit reporting bureaus to look for inaccuracies or opportunities to raise your score. Credit scores are used by loan providers, car insurers, landlords and others to determine what they'll sell you and at what price.

131. **Don't forget about those little nuisance debts.** Small debts can have a large impact on our scores if they go unpaid and get

passed on to a collections agency. Newer credit scoring models ignore debts of less than $100, but not all lenders use the latest models.

132. **Sign up for bank and credit alerts.** Signing up for bank and credit texts or email alerts can help you stay on top of your finances. If there are any fraudulent charges, you'll get notified right away. If someone opens a new credit account in your name, it can trigger an alert. You can also sign up for alerts with your bank. I have these in place and have promptly received alerts when my card was used fraudulently. This idea can save you time and money.

DEBT

133. **Carefully evaluate whether to refinance federal student loans.** Refinancing federal student loans can lead to lower interest rates, which can save borrowers money. Be aware, though, after refinancing with a private lender, borrowers are not eligible for federal payment plans based on income or forgiveness programs.

134. **Consolidate your private student loans.** Interest rates are very low right now. Depending on the type of loans you have, it could be worthwhile to consolidate your student loans into one low-rate package. It's just one way to reduce the burden of student loans, but consider the various student loan consolidation packages available and see what you might save. Even a 1% reduction on a $10,000 loan saves you $100 a year, and your loan is probably

bigger than that (and the rate cut you could get is probably bigger).

135. **Make bi-weekly student loan payments.** If your financial situation allows, look to increase the frequency of your student loan payments. For most loans, interest accrues daily. In order to combat this, you can make bi-weekly student loan payments. Instead of making one monthly payment, cut that in half and pay it every two weeks. You'll save money on interest this way.

136. **Put your student loans on an automatic repayment plan.** Many student loans offer a small rate reduction if you sign up for their automatic debt repayment plan. This way, not only do you save a few bucks a month, you don't have to go to the effort of actually paying the bill either.

137. **Consider paying your mortgage payments bi-weekly rather than monthly.** This lets you painlessly make an extra payment each year, which can add up quickly in the form of reduced life of loan interest payments and increased home equity!

138. **Look to consolidate your debts and lower interest paid.** Talk to a financial advisor or debt counselor about options regarding your situation. You may find that consolidating multiple high-interest payments into one lower interest payment is an effective debt management strategy. This will improve your cash flow and save your interest costs. The average US household with credit card debt has a balance of approximately $16,000, and the average interest rate is likely over 15%. That means Americans are throwing away millions of dollars each month on interest charges, while they overpay with a credit card for purchases they should not be making.

139. **Practice the cardinal rule of having credit cards**—don't pay interest on credit cards. This is obvious but, as soon as you fail to pay off your balance each month, you will be hit with the high rates of interest (e.g., over 15%) that eat away at your monthly budget. If you cannot resist using your available credit, seek help to control your spending. If not, it is likely you will always be in debt.

140. **Avoid financing purchases.** Delaying instant gratification by saving for purchases before buying will a build excellent long-term money habit. This element of self-discipline may be one of the oldest, simplest and most base elements of financial success. Avoid financing and save for things before you buy them. It will allow you to avoid the high cost of installment debt.

141. **Shop around for the right car loan.** Auto loan interest rates can vary greatly depending on the type of institution lending the money, and choosing the right institution can help you secure the lowest rates. Large banks are the leading purveyors of auto loans. Credit unions, however, tend to provide customers with the lowest rates, and the car dealerships of automakers offer attractive financing options for new cars.

142. **Borrow only what you need.** If you take out a student loan, credit card cash advance or other type of loan, try to only borrow what you need. Sometimes you get approved for much more, but don't let that tempt you. This can help you save money on your debt repayment.

143. **Consolidate your debts using a balance transfer card or personal loan.** If you're carrying debt with a high interest rate and have a good credit score, a balance transfer might be a good

option. Taking advantage of a 0% APR offer can help you pay down your debt and save quite a bit of money on interest. Just make sure to factor in the balance transfer fees and pay down the entire transferred balance during the introductory period, if possible.

144. **Don't buy more car than you need.** Per a January 8, 2020, posting on the LendingTree website, the average monthly car payment in the US is $550 for new vehicles, $393 for used and $452 for leased cars. Americans borrow an average $32,480 for new vehicles and $20,446 for used. Lastly, the average loan term is 69 months for new cars, 35 months for used and 37 months for leased vehicles. You should carefully consider what you are borrowing and for how long. You can save hundreds, if not thousands, of dollars by purchasing a less expensive vehicle with a lower loan balance and a shorter loan term.

145. **Create a visual reminder of your debt.** Visualizing what you owe can help many people put their debt burden into terms that are easy to understand. Creating a progress chart that starts with the amount of debt you have and ends with zero will give you a path to being debt free. Each time you pay down a little bit, fill in a little more of that progress bar.

146. **Design your 'debt snowball.'** The debt snowball method is one way to approach debt repayment. Everyone needs a plan to help them get out of debt. So, sit down and develop your own plan and stick to it. Simply having a plan goes a long way toward putting that plan into action, and paying off debts early is one of the surest ways to put money in your pocket in the long run.

147. **Don't borrow from your 401(k) unless it is your last resort.** Taking a loan from your 401(k) is not the best place to borrow. Taking a 401(k) loan is better than withdrawing money from your account, for which you will pay income taxes and a 10% penalty if you're younger than age 59 1/2. Plus, the loans typically come with a lower interest rate than a traditional loan. If you do take a loan, you are usually prohibited from putting more money into your 401(k) for six months, meaning you'll miss opportunities to make pre-tax contributions that lower your taxable income and the related employer match. Another key consideration is by taking part of your retirement savings out of commission, even temporarily, you'll lose out on significant earnings if markets rise.

148. **Get free debt counseling.** The most widely available help managing your debt is with a Consumer Credit Counseling Services (CCCS) counselor. The CCCS network of non-profit counselors can work with you confidentially and judgement free to help you develop a budget, figure out your options and negotiate with creditors to repay your debts. Best of all, the counseling sessions are free of charge unless you enroll in their debt management program and come with no obligations.

149. **Get organized to avoid missed payments**. If you file your monthly statements under your blankets, in a huge pile or in a round file, its time to get organized. By doing so, you can avoid those late payment penalties, which can be substantial and negatively impact your credit scores.

150. **Use extra or unexpected income to reduce your debt.** If you're paying down debt, such as a credit card, and have a fully funded emergency fund, you should likely use these unexpected dollars

to pay down the debt. If you're debt free, use those extra dollars to top off your emergency fund or begin to save for your fulfilling years.

EDUCATION

151. **It's never too early to start saving for college.** The last thing kids need is more "stuff." When your kids are young, if you have enough clothing, toys and other needs, consider asking for donations to their college fund. This can also be used for newborns. Contribute to an infant's college fund, where it will grow for the next 18 years and be there when it is needed.

152. **Don't pay full price to attend virtual or in-person conferences.** Self-employed people and small-business owners looking to attend industry conferences can save money or even go for free by volunteering or speaking. Book early and, for in-person meetings, split the cost of transportation or accommodations with other attendees. If the conference price is still out of reach, just go to the after parties and networking events— often the most valuable parts of the conference.

153. **Look to graduate ahead of time.** If you're in college, or even a parent with a child in college, you may want to look into a three-year versus a four-year program. By graduating a year earlier, students won't have to pay tuition, university fees and board for a fourth year—which means less money they'll have to pay back.

154. **Take free college classes.** At edx.org, you can access more than 2,500 courses from schools such as Harvard and MIT that are

free. This can be an easy way to improve your work-related skills or learn a new subject.

155. **Test out of college classes.** At certain colleges and universities it's possible to earn a bachelor's degree for less total cost by testing out of required classes at an accredited college. This path requires a lot of self-discipline but can save tens of thousands of dollars.

ENERGY CONSUMPTION

156. **Convert to a gas water heater**. They are more efficient and will save you money in the long run, especially if electricity rates are increasing in your area. Plus, gas water heaters can still work during a power outage!

157. **If you live in an older home, consider replacing your single-pane windows.** According to the US Department of Energy, windows can account for up to 30% of a home's heating costs by allowing heat to escape. Although the initial outlay for new windows may be prohibitive, replacing poorly performing windows will eventually pay for itself.

158. **Install a programmable or smart thermostat.** A programmable thermostat allows you to automatically set the heating or cooling temperature of your home while you are away, when you're asleep and so on, significantly saving on your heating and cooling bills. Many of the new devices can be controlled using your smartphone.

159. **Install CFL or LED light bulbs.** If you've never updated the light bulbs throughout your home, consider switching to either CFLs or, better yet, LEDs. These bulbs are about four times more energy efficient than incandescent bulbs and last for many years. One tip—When comparing bulbs, use the *lumens* number to compare bulbs, not the equivalent wattages. *Lumens* indicate the actual amount of light emitted by the bulb. To create a daylight effect in my home, I prefer the highest *lumens* rating.

160. **Lower the temperature on your hot water heater.** The hot water heater is a major energy drain in most homes accounting for about 18% of energy costs according to the US Department of Energy. The water temperature is often set higher than necessary, plus the heat is constantly lost to the environment meaning you have to burn more energy to keep the water temperature so hot.

161. **Open the windows to allow cool air into your home.** It will likely reduce the temperature of the home and bring clean air into the residence.

162. **Switch the direction of your ceiling fan.** Many people don't know that their ceiling fan can go either clockwise or counter-clockwise thanks to a tiny switch, usually on the side. The angle of the blades mean that the fan is actually more efficient going clock-wise in summer as this pushes a breeze around. Use the counter-clockwise direction in winter to pull heat from the ceiling and around the walls.

163. **Unplug all unused electrical devices as they can be energy hogs.** Are there any electrical devices around the house you rarely use that are always plugged in? Most electronic devices constantly draw a small amount of electricity, called a phantom charge, that

can add up quickly when you consider just how many devices and small appliances you own. To eliminate that usage, unplug any device you use infrequently.

164. **Use warm fabrics in winter to save on heating costs.** Instead of turning up the heat on cold winter nights, use flannel sheets (which are warmer than cotton sheets), wear flannel pajamas and add down duvets that will ensure you stay warm and cozy.

165. **Actually use your dishwasher.** This is one area where the newly re-engineered appliances deliver savings. It will save you money and energy (not to mention time) over the old-fashioned way of washing by hand. Just be sure to fill up the dishwasher since the appliance uses the same amount of water whether it's full or half empty.

166. **Add additional insulation to your home.** Even without an energy efficiency checkup, you can probably tell if your home needs more insulation. The most likely spot to need it is your attic. Additional insulation can pay for itself within a year or two and then save you money every year after.

167. **Air dry your clothing.** Cut down on energy costs by drying your clothes on a clothesline or rack. They now have clotheslines for inside the home as well. My wife has used racks for years to protect the color and maintain the size of her clothing.

168. **Always change your furnace filters as directed by the product manual.** Keeping your furnace filters clean is important for saving money and maintaining your home's air quality. If you always forget to refresh your filters, consider having them automatically delivered by a service like FilterEasy at www.secondnature.com.

169. **Always keep your freezer full.** Your freezer works much more efficiently if it is full. The cold items help to keep each other cold, and the freezer doesn't have to work as hard. You can use bags of ice to help keep the freezer at capacity if you don't quite have the food to fill it. Make sure you leave about one inch on each side of the interior for better air exchange.

170. **Ask for an energy audit from your electricity provider.** Did you know that many utilities provide an "energy audit"? It's free for them to do and can save you hundreds of dollars. It involves the company checking for "energy leaks" and providing recommendations on how to stop them, like resealing your windows, replacing old and inefficient heaters/air conditioners and more.

171. **Boil water in the microwave, rather than on the stovetop.** Using the microwave to boil water can use up to 50% less energy. If you do need to boil a pot on the stove, make sure you always place the lid on the pot—it keeps you from wasting energy on heat loss.

172. **Buy energy-efficient appliances**. Look for the Energy Star on appliances and consider the annual energy cost before buying. More efficient appliances cost more, but you make up the extra cost and then some over the life of the product. You can enhance this tip's impact with super-efficient options like induction cooktops and high-efficiency washing machines as well. Look to buy more energy-saving devices for the appliances you use the most.

173. **Change your air filters on your heating, ventilation and air conditioning units regularly.** They will run more efficiently and also help improve air quality.

174. **Check for appliances that consume large amounts of energy.** Use an Electricity Usage Monitor to test your electronics to see which ones have been sucking up all the power.

175. **Check your refrigerator seal.** If the fridge is running all the time, it's important to make sure that it's doing so as efficiently as possible. If it's leaking cold air because of an old seal, then it's also leaking money. This do-it-yourself project is a quick, easy way to save money.

176. **Choose a lighter color roof.** You can use lighter color shingles or, if you have a flat roof, there are also white roof coatings. The lighter colors are more energy-efficient than darker color shingles and black roof coatings.

177. **Clean your dryer lint filter before each load.** This will allow your dryer to work more efficiently.

178. **Consider using space heaters, room air conditioners or cooling fans and keep the settings for the rest of the home on energy-saving settings.** If your spouse/partner likes the temperature higher in winter and lower in summer, doing this will save energy costs.

179. **Consider using timers and power strips.** Along those lines, consider utilizing power strips and power timers to turn electrical devices on and off. A power strip with a switch on it, when turned off, blocks the phantom charge on those devices. A timer can automatically turn off the charge going to a power strip (or anything plugged into it) or can feed power to external lighting at a certain time each night. Smart power strips can even manage electricity flow based on a control device. For instance, your DVD

player will only receive power if the TV is already turned on. These are all great ways to eliminate phantom charges on your home electronic equipment at night or when they're not in use.

180. **Dress appropriately for the season.** If you're working from home and now face higher utility bills, you will likely want to adjust that thermostat now that you are paying for your comfort during the workday. No one will judge your home office attire (unless you are attending meetings in your pajamas), so dress comfortably for the season.

181. **Fix those leaky faucets.** This is an easy DIY project that will save you on hot water heating costs. If you've never done it before, you should be able to learn by watching some YouTube how-to videos. The good folks at Home Depot and Lowe's should be able to help you with any hardware you'll need. I swear by the how-to videos. I am not handy, but they have enabled me to do many small home maintenance projects.

182. **Get a rooftop solar water heater.** These aren't very expensive and can pay for themselves in energy savings fairly quickly.

183. **Install a low-flow showerhead to save energy costs.** This quick weekend project will make your shower more efficient, and you won't feel a difference in your water pressure. Low-flow showerheads can save up to a gallon a minute. (Typical shower heads use about 2.1 gallons per minute.)

184. **Look for areas of air leakage.** If your home has a folding attic stair, a whole house fan or air return, a fireplace or a clothes dryer, that may be just what is occurring in your home every day. These

are often overlooked sources of energy loss costing you higher energy bills. Find them and insulate them for savings.

185. **Properly inflate your vehicle tires.** Properly inflated tires can increase fuel economy by up to 3% according to website www.fueleconomy.gov. In addition, tires inflated to the correct pressure last longer and fail less often. If your car doesn't have tire inflation sensors, consider buying a pressure gauge and checking the pressure yourself.

186. **Reuse rainwater with containers.** This is a favorite tip of mine. You can help conserve water (and money) by capturing rain run-off from your roof. You can then use that water for your flowerbeds and garden. You'll find a variety of barrels available online. I suggest you buy one that has a spigot to attach a hose.

187. **Set the proper temperature for your refrigerator.** Set refrigerators to 40°F and freezers to 0°F.

188. **Store your wine collection without the cost of cooling.** Skip buying a pricey wine cooler that needs to be powered at all times. If you have storage room in the corner of a cellar or at the bottom of a cool, dark closet, use that instead. The money you save can go toward building your collection.

189. **Take advantage of natural light for heating and lighting during certain months of the year.**

190. **Take it easy with your thermostat.** Adjust your thermostat depending on the season of the year. Increase your thermostat by one degree in the summer and lower it by one degree in the winter. Just one degree can save you up to 10% or more on your utility bill.

191. **Turn off the dishwasher's heat dry function.** This is energy that doesn't need to be used—just allow the dishes to air dry for 20 to 30 minutes before you put them away.

192. **Turn off the lights.** Keeping the lights on in your home may not be expensive on a per-watt basis, but it does cost money over time. To save as much as you can, turn off lights any time you leave your house or even when you leave the room. Turning off lights when you have plenty of natural sunlight can also help keep your electric bill down over time. The bottom line—if you aren't using a light, turn it off.

193. **Use fans for cooling, to improve airflow and reduce the cost of air conditioning.** They can make it feel up to 4 degrees cooler. When it's hot outside, position a fan to blow air out a window. If you're lucky enough to have a strong wind, set the fan to blow in the same direction to maximize airflow. Close nearby windows to keep exhausted air from flowing back in and open those on the other side of the house (ideally in cool, shaded areas). In a multi-level home, place the fan in a top-floor window and open windows on lower floors, where air is cooler. For windows that catch direct sun, use blackout blinds or heavy drapes to minimize solar heat gain.

194. **Use solar powered lights or LEDs for outdoor lighting.** If your home has an outdoor area with decorative or security lighting, consider using solar powered lights instead of paying for electricity to keep them on all night. If you can't find solar fixtures that work, install LED fixtures to save you money long term.

195. **Use window shades.** During the summer months, close the shades to block out sunlight and open them to let more light in

during the winter months. Tight-fitting, insulating window shades can help to reduce drafts in the winter if other weatherizing measures haven't fixed the problem. In winter, closing your curtains and shades at night can help to keep drafts out, while opening them during the day can help sun warm the house. In summer, close south- and west-facing window shades during the day to keep the sun from over-warming the house.

196. **Use your appliances at night or during off-peak periods.** Run appliances such as clothes dryers and dishwashers at night to avoid peak energy rates and the humid heat they generate. Excess humidity is more than uncomfortable. It can also be expensive since air conditioners use extra energy to process the moisture.

197. **Wash and dry full loads of clothing and dishes to maximize efficiency.**

ENTERTAINMENT

198. **Buy video games that have a lot of replay value and don't acquire new ones until you've mastered what you have.** What's the point in playing a video game just once? My daughter focuses on games that can be played over and over again. Good targets include quest games—they maximize the value of your gaming dollar. Lastly, once you're finished with a game for good, take it to a video game resale shop like GameStop and see if you can trade it in for store credit or use it to purchase another game.

199. **Consider cancelling club memberships.** With the recent pandemic restrictions, this can be a good idea. Look at what you are spending for your gym, local country club or other recreational

activities and make a hard decision as to whether you will use them going forward. On the other hand, you may want to keep them to help the organizations weather the financial impacts of the pandemic.

200. **Create a healthy, open-air outdoor cinema for your family and friends.** With social distancing in mind, create an outdoor movie experience. Have all in attendance bring their own seats and snacks, and you will create a safe night out for everyone.

201. **Cut down on television viewing.** One way some have saved money is to drastically cut down on the amount of television they watch. There are a number of financial and health benefits to doing this, including less exposure to advertising, a lower electric bill and perhaps a lower cable bill if you downgrade your subscription allowing more time to focus on other things in life, such as going outside to take a walk.

202. **Don't spend a lot of money on entertaining very young children.** They won't likely remember that trip to Disney when they are age 3. Instead, give them home-based experiences, including playing ball in the backyard, visiting the local park or planting a garden. These experiences will stay with them. When they are old enough, take that family trip to Disney. Realize that what your children want most of all is time with you.

203. **Get free eBooks to read.** Go to the website Project Gutenberg to access over 60,000 eBooks that you can download for free.

204. **Go outside and take in the fresh air.** The great outdoors is almost always free and, with the added benefit of free exercise, the

outdoors is an incredible resource. During the pandemic, many people began to walk through their neighborhoods and found all sorts of points of interest.

205. **In this pandemic-impacted world, go to the socially distanced drive-in for a movie or show.** Drive-ins allow you to get an economical time out. Taking a carload of your family members to see an event will also be cheaper than paying for individual tickets.

206. **Instead of cutting the cable cord completely, just cancel the cable or satellite channels you don't watch.** Many people with cable services are often paying for a premium package that they don't really need. For the longest time, my wife and I were subscribed to movie channels we did not use. We decided it was easier and cheaper to just pay for the movies we wanted to watch.

207. **Invite friends over for a socially distanced event instead of spending money to go out.** It is always cheaper to stay in with friends and come up with your own entertainment. My daughter sponsors game nights, murder mystery events and movie nights. Everyone in attendance brings food and beverages or she collects a small cover charge to pay for these items.

208. **Join a volunteer program.** Volunteering is a meaningful way to spend your free time that allows you to meet new people, get some exercise and involve yourself in a positive project that can lift your spirits. It usually doesn't cost much and can provide a lot of entertainment and a fulfilling day when you're in the right mindset. I have done this with Habitat for Humanity a number of times. You also might learn something, and the physical exercise is an added benefit.

209. **Look to eliminate your cable bill.** You can usually find cheaper, but less convenient ways, to gain access to your favorite shows if you look hard enough. Or you can save money by only having an Internet package that offers a growing number of streaming services.

210. **Meet for breakfast or lunch instead of dinner.** If you're overdue for a catch-up with friends or you're looking for a more budget-friendly date with your other half, consider going out for breakfast or lunch instead of dinner. It's usually much cheaper.

211. **Read more.** According to the Bureau of Labor Statistics, the average adult reads only 10 minutes per day compared to spending over 2 hours per day on social media. Reading is one of the cheapest and most beneficial hobbies around. Most towns have a library available to the public—visit and check out some books that interest you. The Internet and services such as Google and Amazon Prime can provide you with more than enough subject matter to keep you engaged. You'll learn something new, improve your reading ability, enjoy yourself and do it all for free.

212. **Seek out less costly entertainment options.** This would include looking for local free art shows, festivals, performances and exhibitions. Look for websites for the area you live in. You may be surprised with what you find available for little or no cost.

213. **Share entertainment with family and friends.** Similar to swapping clothes, ask to borrow DVDs and CDs or share the payments for a joint streaming account. If you share streaming, just make sure you both agree on how and when account payments will be made.

214. **Spend less to see movies.** Once movie theaters reopen, you can save money by buying tickets in bulk at warehouse clubs or straight from theater chains, by attending matinees or by going on discount days and avoiding the overpriced snack bar.

215. **Stream movies for cheap or for free.** Instead of paying for a pay-per-view or movie ticket, stream one from your Amazon, Netflix or Hulu accounts. Many libraries now have movies on DVD and Blu-ray that patrons can check out. Also, check whether your phone or cable provider offers free streaming, like how Comcast offers Peacock or Verizon provides a year of Disney+. Also take advantage of free trial periods, such as Netflix or Hulu for a month. Apple also offers one year of Apple TV+ with the purchase of any Apple device.

216. **Try a "staycation."** In these times of pandemic uncertainty, you may really need a break from your daily routine. Instead of taking your family to the islands, try being a tourist in your own city. Not only will this keep you safer, it will save you hundreds (or potentially thousands) of dollars. You can also explore your area with fresh eyes and have some fun while doing it.

217. **Utilize free online courses or webinars as much as you can.** You can save money on tuition, fees and transportation by using the ever-growing inventory of online educational content available. If you want to spend a little, splurge on the Greatest Courses available on Amazon Video.

218. **Visit your state's historic sites.** Every state has an often-ignored history. Look up the national monuments, historic estates, forts, battlegrounds and historic buildings. Many of these sites can be visited for no admission fee. For the most accurate information

on where to go and what to see, contact the historical society closest to your destination.

219. **Take a job at your favorite place.** If you already spend a lot of time at sporting events or at the bar down the street, become a referee, vendor or bartender on the weekends and you will save money on game tickets and drinks. Turn your entertainment time into a source of cash.

220. **Buy a smart watch and get more exercise.** To get my calorie burn each day, I track my walking and running activities. A good smart watch and activity application will track your exercise results and calorie burn. This can become a great health habit and will likely save on doctor visits long term.

221. **Switch to eBooks from printed versions.** While I've mentioned before how the cheapest way to get books is for free from your library, that's not always an option for everyone. While this may not be the most inexpensive thing on this list, it can save you a ton of money if you love reading. Electronic versions of books are usually cheaper than those in print.

222. **Create your own home theater.** Turn at-home movie watching into your own mini cinema. Make popcorn, put in a soda fountain, mandate a smartphone-free zone and decorate the area with old movie posters or ones created by your family.

223. **Drink alcohol before going out or BYOB if it is permitted.** This is a practice used in some of the Scandinavian countries. Having a few drinks before you go out can save you a ton at bars and restaurants. Before putting this tip into practice, make sure you or

your group has designated a driver who will be responsible for safely transporting your party to and from your destination(s).

224. **Go camping.** Looking for some peace and quiet? Go camping! It's an affordable way to travel and can get you back to being at one with nature. It has also been shown to be calming and a great way to deal with stress.

225. **Go to museums on free days.** Many museums around the world have free days, mornings or afternoons on certain days of the week and at certain times of the year. Some have "by donation" days as well. So, get your museum fix by going on the free or pay-what-you-can days.

226. **Ignore pricey workout clothes.** I know this one is unacceptable to some people. But you don't need that $200 yoga outfit. Lululemon and Athleta may be in vogue, but frugal people can turn to plenty of places for deals on workout clothes. Check out websites such as The Clymb, ClothingUnder10.com, and Steep&Cheap, or inexpensive retailers such as Old Navy.

227. **Subscribe to selected print magazines**. If you prefer regularly reading a print copy of a publication, it is usually cheaper to subscribe rather than buy individual issues. Amazon also offers some great deals on personal finance magazines (search personal finance). Prime members get access to a few magazines per month as part of the membership.

228. **Take your family to local outdoor venues.** If you have reached the saturation point with streaming, video games and you have watched all of your favorite movies—get outside! Whether you decide to stay local or travel a distance, drive off to the closest

national park and venture into the outside world. You can save money and get some fresh air at the same time. There are millions of trails and walkways to explore.

229. **The local library is your friend.** Before you buy books online, visit your friendly local library to see if you can borrow titles of interest. Most libraries also have CDs, audiobooks and digital copies of your favorite books for rent at reasonable rates.

230. **Use Goldstar for entertainment deals.** You can get entertainment for a fraction of the cost using a site like Goldstar. You can buy tickets to concerts, sports games, theater shows and more at a discount. You can also find similar deals on Groupon.

FINANCIAL

231. **Check on your Social Security benefits.** I know many people, particularly younger adults, who do not believe they will ever collect Social Security retirement benefits. I wouldn't write-off these benefits just yet. Instead, you should stay on top of what you qualify for. To do this, you should set up an online account. Once you've done so, identity thieves will be unable to create a fraudulent account in your name and use it to apply for benefits. In addition, you can check your earnings history against your W-2 forms or tax returns to make sure there are no errors or gaps in your earnings record that could reduce your Social Security benefits. You can also look up estimated retirement, disability and survivor benefits and, in certain cases, request a replacement Social Security card. To set up an account, simply go to www.ssa.gov/myaccount, follow the prompts and answer the questions.

232. **Consider joining a credit union.** Credit unions are non-profit financial institutions that are owned cooperatively by their members (i.e., people with an account at the credit union). They offer many of the same services as banks but usually give more attractive terms and share their profits with members. Fees and interest rates may be lower on credit cards and loans, and checking and savings accounts may pay higher interest compared with other financial services firms.

233. **Insist on no-fee banking services.** Switch your accounts to a bank with fee-free checking and ATM use or fee reimbursement—often available from smaller local banks or credit unions. These institutions also typically offer checking accounts with no minimums and lower fees than the big institutions. Your best opportunity to save is with the online services from CapitalOne, Charles Schwab, Ally Bank or USAA Bank (for members and relatives of military members and veterans). I have used CapitalOne for years.

234. **Learn about the full range of benefits your company offers.** Spend some time on your company's website or with an HR person at work learning about all the benefits available to you. You may find benefits that will surprise you and save you money. These could include subsidies for working at home, cell phone discount plans, student loan repayment options and plans to reduce legal, health and caregiving costs. Following a sit-down with someone at work, I gained access to free tickets to sporting events, entertainment venues and a discount on my cell phone costs.

235. **See if you are eligible for state and city tax credits.** Search for the name of your state or city and the word "tax credit." Some states and/or lower jurisdictions offer tax credits for eligible individuals.

236. **Move your bank accounts to take advantage of benefits, rewards and higher interest rates.** If you're paying a monthly fee for your checking or savings account, you would benefit from researching some of newest banking offers out there. Not only do some of the best banks offer sign-up bonuses simply for opening an account and setting up direct deposit, but some offer attractive interest rates to new customers as well.

237. **Create a financial cookie jar.** Set up a cookie jar to capture those little handfuls of change you come home with. Put the change away every month. At the end of the year you will have money for holiday shopping or, as my mom used to do, a source of money in a pinch if one of the kids needs something at school or for gas money when they are older.

238. **Stop giving the government an interest free loan with your income taxes.** If you get a tax refund every year, you're doing it wrong. Stop lending your money to the government each year interest free and save interest for yourself. When you receive a tax refund, you paid too much in taxes over the year and they are giving you your money back. Think of it this way. You technically gave the government extra money all year for free. Yes, you got your money back, but that was a free loan. It is better to take your money back and earn interest on it by reducing the amount of taxes you pay during the year. Speak with your accountant to

ensure you don't pay too little and end up with a large tax bill at the end of the year.

239. **Utilize online bill pay with your bank or credit card company by setting all your recurring bills on automatic payments.** Never pay a late fee again. Set up everything you can on automatic payment. It may also improve your credit scores. This saves you money on stamps and paper checks by allowing you to just fill in an online form, click submit and have your bill paid. I hardly use checks and stamps anymore.

240. **Get your annual income taxes done for free.** Do you really need a professional tax preparer to file your taxes? Visit the Internal Revenue Service's free file website where they list recommended free tax filing programs. Also, pay attention to your community flyers as accounting industry members often offer free income tax filing services to certain people who may need them.

241. **Read personal finance books and blogs.** If you want to change your life, then I recommend that you spend two hours per week improving your money knowledge and skills. Go to the Spend2 tab of the financialverse.com website for my suggestions on how to spend that two hours and what resources you can access to improve your money knowledge.

242. **Try to do your own income taxes.** For most people, this is a task they can do using today's reasonably priced tax return preparation apps. I personally use Turbo Tax and have done so for over a decade. These applications will walk you through the process of completing the returns and will ask all of the necessary questions to make sure you do not miss reporting any required information. For example, the applications will take you through all

deductions to make sure you get every deduction to which you are entitled. They also run through all sources of income to report. For most people, preparing their own return or just answering the questions needed to complete the return will be an eye-opening experience. It will significantly increase their awareness of tax-related issues and how to reduce their tax bill.

243. **Take advantage of the major middle class tax breaks of IRAs, 401(k)s, Health Savings Accounts and 529 or College Savings plans.** Become familiar with each of these tax breaks, how you qualify and how to use them. They were created to help individuals improve their financial lives.

244. **Understand the special tax rules for self-employed people.** If you are self-employed, there are special rules that you should discuss with a tax professional. For example, these rules may allow you to deduct certain expenses and make larger contributions to retirement savings plans.

245. **Understand the tax basics of major deductions and components of income.** Everyone should learn the basics about the special tax treatment of medical expenses, college loan interest, tuition payments and continuing education costs. There are special provisions that can benefit you.

FOOD

246. **Buy generic or store brands when you can.** Many products (not just food) are available in a store brand or generic form for significantly less money. Before I commit to a large purchase of a store brand or generic, I buy a small sample and have my family

test it to make sure they are okay with it. This includes everything from paper towels to maple syrup.

247. **Plan ahead and spend one day cooking and freezing meals for multiple days to reduce preparation time and meal cost.**

248. **Don't pay for your kid's meals.** If you do dine out during the week, make sure you visit one of the many places that offer "kids eat free" specials. At least you won't be paying for their meals.

249. **Freeze in-season food for use later.** Buy fresh fruits and vegetables in season for the lowest prices and best flavor. Then you can use them later for a treat. My mom used to do this with New Jersey peaches and tomatoes each year.

250. **Reduce unnecessary food spoilage.** We read that Americans waste a significant amount of food. This is due, in part, to many people misunderstanding that "best buy" dates indicate the last day of peak quality, not safety. Many foods are still safe to eat days, sometimes weeks, after the date on the package. Be sure to take a second look at the food inside the package before tossing it.

251. **Stick to a firm list when you go shopping.** We have all heard the familiar story that someone went to Target or Trader Joe's for one thing and ended up with a cart full of things they might eat but don't need right now. That's why it's good to use the Notes app on your smartphone to make a list that you can cross off and stick to.

252. **Make sure your grocery list is carefully planned.** Few things are as aggravating as getting excited about cooking to save money, ringing up your groceries and realizing your $62 receipt only covers you for a limited number of meals. Try to buy only the groceries you need (versus snacks, alcohol, appetizers, etc.). If there are

ingredients that you can plausibly skip (like fresh herbs or an out-of-season vegetable that you can easily swap), consider doing that too.

253. **Use the food in your freezer, pantry and storage.** As we have seen during the pandemic, it can be a mistake to stockpile too much food and not have the chance to use it before the expiration dates. If you find yourself with a full refrigerator or pantry, reconsider your grocery shopping plan and adjust downward. Avoid waste by planning your meals around what is already available in your freezer or pantry. Mix and match stored food with fresh food to keep your meals palatable.

254. **When you eat out consider having "linner."** Linner is when you have a hearty late lunch and a smaller dinner. In most areas of the country, the cost of a restaurant lunch is substantially less than dinner.

255. **Become your household's barista.** If you are a fan of the more sophisticated brews, learning to make them at home can save you money and allow you to continue to enjoy your favorites. If you consider the cost of a good coffee machine and a bag of beans every few weeks along with some milk, you'll easily be saving more than $1,000 each year compared to a daily purchase at Starbucks. It is your choice—savings versus convenience.

256. **Bring your breakfast and lunch from home if you are working in an office location.** Eating out daily adds up very quickly. Even a relatively cheap breakfast and lunch could easily add up to $15 per day—that's $75 a week! This will also reduce your virus exposure in public locations.

257. Buy cast iron kitchen utensils. These investments will serve you for a lifetime. A cast-iron skillet is indispensable for far more than its expected uses. Reach for one when making roast chicken, upside-down cake, cornbread and even pizza (just flip the pan over and use the bottom as a pizza stone).

258. Check out bulk stores for more savings. Many foods can be bought in bulk for way less at stores such as Sam's Club or Costco. For instance, you can buy frozen vegetables cheaply in large quantities. Or buy your paper goods from a bulk store to save. Be sure to buy only the products your family intends to use. Too often people stock up on large quantities of items they use infrequently.

259. Commit to eating or ordering out one less time each month. After the pandemic eating restrictions pass, consider saving money without sacrificing your lifestyle. Take small steps to reduce your dining budget. Start off with reducing how often you eat out or order out just once per month.

260. Consider eating more vegetables. Vegetables are, on average, cheaper than meats. It certainly is not practical for a family to suddenly switch from meat-based meals to vegetarian meals just to save money. However, making vegetables a larger part of each meal, or even planning one vegetarian meal per week, is not out of reach for most families.

261. Consider starting an edible garden. Instead of spending money to maintain a beautiful yard full of flowers, spend the money tending a garden that you can eat. What and when you can grow things will vary based on where you live.

262. **Consider using powders or concentrates for your favorite drinks.** Instead of buying prepared products, you can make iced tea or juice a lot cheaper at home.

263. **Consider what you are spending dining out.** According to the US Bureau of Labor Statistics, the average American household spent over $3,500 dining out in 2019. This is 43% of a typical household's food spend. When you decide to eat out, you can save money by being aware of your options. Order an appetizer as your main course. They are generally more than large enough to satisfy your appetite and will be much cheaper than the entrées. Another option is to split an entrée. Even if the restaurant charges you for the split (as some do), this will still be a cheaper option than both of you getting your own meal. My wife and I do this, especially at restaurants with exceptionally large portions.

264. **Create a neighborhood cooking group.** If you're close with your neighbors, consider creating a cooking group. Each family in the group cooks dinner one night per week for the other families in the group. This way you can enjoy a few nights off from cooking, as well as added savings from buying cooking items in bulk.

265. **Cut meal costs by choosing restaurants with free drink refills.** Many fast food and casual restaurants offer those wonderful unlimited drink refills. Chains with this perk have included Taco Bell, Chipotle, Five Guys, Olive Garden, McDonald's and In-N-Out.

266. **Dine out for special occasions only.** In this pandemic restricted world we live in only dine out for special occasions. You could get several days worth of food at the grocery store for the same

amount that you pay for a single dinner out for one person at an upscale restaurant.

267. **Do your shopping during the week.** Industry data suggests that prices are lower during the week than on weekends. I have read that Wednesday is the best day for low prices with shopping earlier in the day yielding the best prices.

268. **Don't buy wine based on ratings alone.** Never buy a wine just because it received a high score in a magazine. Good press can raise the price. A lesser score doesn't necessarily mean a wine is inferior. Research your wine purchases and you can save money.

269. **Don't shop hungry—a cardinal rule!** I swear by this idea. You are likely to spend more when hungry because your eyes and stomach will be doing the shopping, not your brain.

270. **Eat a balanced breakfast.** I have learned how important this is as you manage stress, weight and your overall health. It will help you reduce unnecessary and expensive snacking. Eating a healthy breakfast fills you up with energy for the day while also curbing your desire for a costly snack or a big, expensive lunch. A bowl of oatmeal or a protein rich egg bowl in the morning is often the one thing that keeps me from running out to eat an expensive lunch later in the day. Try to eat at least a 500-calorie breakfast.

271. **Eat in season and locally.** You may know that certain out-of-season fruits can cost you an arm and a leg. Reacquaint yourself with your local growing season. The cheapest way to buy produce is to get only what is naturally growing in your area. That doesn't mean you have to start shopping at farmers' markets (which can sometimes be more expensive just for the quaintness factor), it just

means that you purchase the produce that is abundant in your area at that particular time.

272. **Eat less meat by going meatless one or two days per week.** Meat is very expensive when you consider its nutritional value, especially compared to vegetables and fruits. In almost every case, protein-packed staples like beans offer a much better value. In addition, eating less meat helps protect the environment by creating fewer pollutants.

273. **Minimize the food you waste.** It's great to stock up on fresh fruits and veggies to stay healthy; but, if you always end up tossing something in the trash each week, try to reassess. To prevent the waste, switching to frozen produce is a great idea (like frozen berries, spinach or stir-fry veggies).

274. **Get free eggs.** Four chickens on a quarter acre of land provide free eggs, natural insect control and free fertilizer. My youngest daughter has friends who live in a rural area who swear by this idea. They no longer pay the price for free-range eggs at the grocery store.

275. **Go old school for bargains.** Even in a digital world, grocers still compete for your business and use some print materials to get you to buy. Check flyers or those weekly local ads you get in the mail and shop local for some bargains.

276. **In this pandemic-cautioned world consider getting your groceries delivered.** Using online ordering services such as Amazon Fresh and Instacart help to limit impulse purchases and protect you from exposure to COVID-19.

277. **Instead of buying bottled juices or doing a pricey, prepackaged cleanse, use a home juicer.** The time commitment and cleanup are not for everyone. So, only buy a cheap juicer or a used one and upgrade if juicing becomes an ongoing thing.

278. **Invest in a deep freezer.** If you have the space in your home, buying a deep freezer (new or used) can be a great bargain to help reduce food costs, but only if you use it. Often, having some extra freezer space allows you to buy in bulk and pay lower prices overall. Even better, you can store a number of prepared meals enabling you to just go home and pop something homemade (and cheap) in the oven.

279. **Invest in a second refrigerator.** I have done this for years and it saves money. We have ours in our garage and we use it to cool beverages and to keep an extra supply of frequently eaten foods such as yogurt and bread products.

280. **Learn to braise.** There are two ways to get tender meat: buy tender cuts or buy tougher cuts at a fraction of the price and cook them to tenderness. Get out that old cookbook and learn how to braise low-priced chuck or stew meat, along with overflow veggies, for a delicious low-cost meal.

281. **Leverage deals at Amazon.com and Walmart.com.** Keep an eye out for specials. Stock up when the conditions are right.

282. **Make bulk purchases of non-perishable items.** Many people never bother to look at some of the larger packages of non-perishable items–they think overall it's just too much. Try looking at the cost per unit of all of the sizes and choose the one that's the best deal. Make sure you check the "use by" dates to give you the

leeway to consume the larger quantities you are purchasing. You can always store extra paper products for use later.

283. **Make sure your freezer is big enough for your household.** Buying or cooking in bulk ahead of time can be a godsend if you're trying to save both time and money. To do this properly, you often need to freeze your food to preserve it for the week. If you have one small freezer, this may not be possible.

284. **Make your own beer or wine.** If you enjoy an occasional drink, this is a great way to enjoy some of your favorite beverages at a steep discount. You can easily make five gallons of beer or wine at once, and it doesn't take that long once you've mastered the process. Even better, it's a great activity to do with friends. Some nice entertainment plus some free beverages—that's a great frugal deal.

285. **Only buy organic items that are essential.** Buying everything organic isn't always financially feasible. Restrict your purchases to items most likely to have higher pesticide residues: apples, bell peppers, celery, cherries, grapes (imported), lettuce, nectarines, peaches, pears, potatoes, spinach and strawberries. It's also wise to buy organic meat and dairy products that don't contain growth hormones.

286. **Pay attention to expiration dates when you shop.** Haven't we all gotten home from shopping and discovered some item that we bought has an expired date on it. We may have grand illusions about returning to the store and demanding a replacement or a refund, but we don't make it back to the store. It's much easier to just keep a close eye on expiration dates as you put the items in your cart. Similarly, double check that the carton of eggs you're

choosing is free of cracked eggs, that the cans you've chosen are not dented and everything in a jar is well sealed.

287. **Pay attention to unit costs.** The one caveat about buying food in bulk is to keep an eye on the unit cost of anything you buy. Most grocery stores offer a unit price listing so that you can compare apples to apples (so to speak), but some do not. Get in the habit of carrying a calculator with you to the grocery store (or using the calculator function on your cell phone) to figure out what product gives you the biggest bang for your buck.

288. **Plan your shopping trips.** If you plan your grocery shopping carefully, you can significantly reduce your costs for several reasons: (1) check what you have on the shelf to avoid unnecessary purchases; (2) make a list of what you need to buy to avoid impulse shopping; (3) buy items in bulk when it makes sense for the size of your family; (4) comparison shop to get the best value for your money. For instance, in my area Publix offers good value over the specialty markets for fruits, vegetables and meats.

289. **Save on coffee beans.** Use half of your used coffee beans in the next batch. Repeat this cycle and you'll only use half the recommended scoop each time. Some coffee drinkers swear by this method.

290. **Save on your wine purchases.** Wines often cost more when they come from a well-known wine-making region or are made from a popular grape. Rather than heading straight for a familiar bottle, try something different. Instead of Chardonnay, Cabernet Sauvignon or Merlot, try Albarino, Malbec or Sangiovese. Chile, New Zealand, Australia and South Africa are also

wine-producing countries that make good quality bargain wines. I personally like Malbecs.

291. **Shredded or sliced food is very costly.** You can save significant food dollars by doing your own shredded cheese or slicing your own fruit. You pay far less for a block of cheese and get far more in total. It only takes a few minutes to grate the entire block, and it's well worth the savings. The same applies for fruit, like melons. Sure, it's easier to just buy it in a packet or container. But it's not that much harder to buy actual melons and spend a few minutes slicing them when you get home.

292. **Switch to a SodaStream or a Drinkmate system.** If you drink a lot of carbonated water, making your own sodas can save you big dollars. Mix in fresh fruit or mint for natural flavoring.

293. **Switch to drinking water with your meals versus soft drinks or alcoholic beverages.** A soft drink at a restaurant can add $2-$3 to your tab. Buying sodas for your home is not much cheaper either. Another idea is to add a water filter to your water source, tap or a filter pitcher to your fridge to reduce soft drink consumption.

294. **Take advantage of happy hour specials.** If your local watering hole has reopened, visit when they provide free snacks. Pretty much every bar that serves food has happy hour specials. It's a smart way to eat and drink while saving on expense. Post pandemic some establishments have to provide food as part of their offerings.

GIFTING

295. **Give the gift of time.** Time is one of the most precious things we each have. For those near and dear to you, consider giving them the gift of an outing or activity with you. An outing, a lunch, a dinner or even a quick cup of coffee could be worth more to a person than an actual gift. They will appreciate the gesture and, in this day and age, understand its importance.

296. **Join American Greeting Cards for gift cards.** For a bi-annual fee of $29.99 you can send all the eCards you need to your friends and family. This saves dramatically over the cost of paper cards. I use this service and the card selection has been excellent.

297. **Save for the holidays.** Holiday spending can really be an issue for many households. It is a great idea to save ahead of time for the amounts to be spent or make purchases in advance of the holiday season. Most importantly, stick to your holiday spending budget to avoid the January credit card headache many people encounter. You can often get nice gifts for *next* Christmas in January. Buying throughout the year can help you feel less pressure during the holiday season and can save you a fortune.

298. **Save money on packing supplies.** Don't toss away all the wrapping paper that once covered your birthday or holiday presents. Instead, run it through your paper shredder (cut to size first, if needed) or tear it into pieces and crumple them up. Use this paper for lining gift boxes or protecting breakables to be shipped.

299. **Agree to limit gift giving**. At Christmas we all have a tendency to go overboard when it comes to gift giving. To cut back, many

families agree to limits on amounts to be spent with extended family, which really helps save money for everyone.

300. **Create handwritten cards for all occasions.** I really appreciate getting something written by hand these days. Another idea is to create cards using new photos you have taken or old pictures taken during family occasions.

301. **Do some holiday shopping right after the holidays.** Some people do this right after the Christmas holiday, but it is a strategy that works year-round. You can buy gifts, gift wrap or gift bags at large savings. The discounts are tremendous, and you can just put this stuff in the closet until next year.

302. **Get creative with your wrapping paper.** This idea comes from my daughter. The most unique and beautiful wrapping paper— vintage scarves, newspaper, colorful cloth and more—is already lying around your house. Reusing such materials saves money and helps the environment.

303. **Give an experience as a gift to your teenage children.** There's so much pressure to make sure that there's a pile of gifts under the tree each year that everyone seems to ignore the huge cost involved. Despite the fact that people often forget exactly what they received. Your teenagers will remember, however, that time they went skiing together or the trip to Yellowstone. Depending on your family interests, you can typically discover an unlimited number of options for experiences that you can do.

304. **Keep kids' birthday parties simple.** Today's social media-influenced culture has a lot to answer for in terms of our budgets— that includes kids' birthday parties. You absolutely don't need the

over-the-top circus or clown-inspired parties that we often see online. Keep it simple and authentic and the celebrations will be more meaningful for everyone.

305. **Send inexpensive flowers.** Chrysanthemums and carnations and alstroemerias cost less than roses and last longer. No matter the type of flowers, call a local florist near the recipient instead of ordering online. The florist may offer savings or prepare a better bouquet for the same price.

306. **Shop for a diamond gift online.** Looking for a diamond ring for that special someone? Get a good price by shopping online and knowing the five Cs: clarity, color, cut, carat and certification. Don't compromise on cut, which makes a diamond sparkle, but a low clarity or color grade is harder to notice and can make a large stone more affordable. Also, consider alternative synthetic diamonds or alternative gemstones.

307. **Stock up on gifts for kids' birthday parties.** Toys go on sale every January. Use this time of year to stock up on a variety of inexpensive gifts. Keep a stockpile and add to it whenever you spot a good deal. Set a limit for yourself, such as no more than $5 or $10. When the inevitable party invitation arrives, visit your stockpile instead of the store.

308. **Take $20 or more per week and deposit it into a sinking fund account for gift giving.** This is one way to discipline yourself so that you don't have the big, expensive credit card bill coming in January each year. If you put $20 per week away, you will have $1,000 put aside for holiday shopping.

HEALTHCARE

309. Consider giving up the habit of smoking and/or vaping. Think of the health benefits. After decades of Surgeon General warnings, a lot of people still haven't gotten the message. The average national price of a pack of cigarettes was over $6 in the first quarter of 2020. If you smoke a pack a day, you're spending $180 a month. That's $2,160 a year going up in smoke. If a person starts at age 18 and doesn't kick the habit until they are 50, they will spend (assuming the price doesn't go up, which it will) almost $70,000 on cigarettes.

310. Look to buy generic or store-brand drugs instead of brand name medicines for your prescriptions and over-the-counter purchases.

311. Shop around for costly medical procedures. Believe it or not, you can check the rates for various procedures at hospitals just like you can check insurance rates. If your doctor has recommended a procedure, find out the current procedural terminology (CPT) code for that procedure. This is the standard billing code that will be the same across the industry. With that code in hand, you can contact the billing department to find out the cost of the procedure—this could take some persistence. If another hospital charges less for the procedure, ask your original hospital if it will match that price. You will be surprised what you can save by doing this.

312. Always ask your doctor questions. It is your body and you need to know what is going on. Being your own advocate is an important part of medicine. When your doctor recommends a procedure or a medication, be sure to ask questions. Find out why the doctor believes it's necessary and whether there are alternative treatments. Blindly following what your doctor recommends might be costly and possibly unnecessary.

313. **Don't skimp on preventive healthcare appointments.** I cannot emphasize how important this is. Routine dental checkups, for example, help prevent fillings, root canals and dental crowns—all of which are expensive and no fun. Eye exams and an annual physical examination can detect heath issues before they become major concerns.

314. **Enroll in a Flexible Spending Account.** If your employer offers a flexible spending account, consider electing one. For 2020 you can contribute up to $2,750; however, you won't have the benefit of being able to retain the funds for future investment. If they're not used during the tax year or by March 31 after the tax year ends, you forfeit the funds. I always projected what my FSA eligible expenses would be for the next year to make sure my contributions were as close as possible to what I planned on spending. Fsastore.com is a great source of information for flexible spending accounts and offers over 4,000 items guaranteed to be covered, so you can shop knowing that what you buy will paid for with your flexible spending dollars.

315. **Get your prescriptions through the mail.** Investigate whether or not your health insurer offers the purchase and delivery of your prescriptions by mail. I get one of my prescriptions this way and receive a 90-day supply for one deductible. Try it; you may save money. You will also avoid the trip to the pharmacy. Setting this up online will also save time.

316. **Proactively reduce your medical bills.** If you have a hospital bill, contact the billing department and ask if you can get a discount for paying cash or if you can pay a lower amount. Often they'll be happy that they're collecting at least a portion of the bill and may be willing to cut a large percentage (e.g., 10-20%) off your amount.

317. **Take advantage of your company's wellness program and related benefits.** Check with your employer to see what wellness benefits are available. These benefits range from discounted gym memberships to access to websites offering resources to keep you healthy and happy.

318. **Try to keep your doctors in-network.** Anytime your primary doctor refers you to a specialist, make sure the services are in-network with your insurance provider. If they aren't, ask your doctor if there is another specialist they can recommend. For surgeries, check to make sure the facility and the anesthesiologist are in-network providers as well. This will save you the higher deductibles and coinsurance amounts you will pay for out-of-network care.

319. **Adjust your lifestyle choices to save money.** Look at your lifestyle activities and see where you can cut back. Recreational drug use, smoking and drinking are areas where adults should not be spending money. These can be self-destructive habits that can ruin your health and that of your family as well. Instead of spending money on these items, think about how much money you would have in your investments if you divert the funds to other assets. In this day and age of health-conscious living, recreational drug use, alcohol consumption and smoking have no place in the household and its best to put these habits to rest.

320. **Ask about discounts, coupons and samples for medication.** If you are not able to get a generic version of your medication, you still might be able to save money. Ask your doctor to write you a prescription for three months worth of a regular medication, which generally means you will only have to pay one co-pay instead of three. Ask if they offer any coupons. Alternatively, many doctors will try to help out their patients by giving them samples of expensive meds. Ask your doctor if there are samples available that you can use to help reduce your medication costs.

321. **Comparison shop for prescription drugs.** Don't just rely on the closest drugstore because the cost to you can vary significantly from pharmacy to pharmacy. Make sure to check out your local pharmacist, supermarkets, wholesale clubs and mail-order pharmacies. There are also a number of good apps available to help you reduce the cost of medicines. I have used GoodRX.com to save money. The app shows you which neighborhood pharmacies offer the best prices.

322. **Don't let your doctor be a stranger.** Be sure to understand and make use of the free wellness care options in your health insurance policy. Even healthy individuals need to see their doctors regularly. Making sure that you get your regular physicals, lab work or tests will help to catch any potential health problems before they become major matters in your life.

323. **Have your hospital bill itemized.** Because of the number of people involved in any one patient's care—nurses, doctors, specialists, etc.—the rate of errors on hospital bills is relatively high. Any time you have to pay for a hospital stay, request an itemized bill

and ask questions about any items you do not understand and be sure to dispute any errors.

324. **Manage your stress.** Stress can lead to a lot of additional expenses related to medical costs, stress spending, stress eating and more. So, manage your stress. This way you can keep your expenses in check.

325. **Open a Health Savings Account, if eligible.** One of the best ways to deal with high out-of-pocket costs is to open a Health Savings Account. For 2020 you can contribute up to $3,550 to a plan for a single individual and $7,100 for a family. HSAs have four primary advantages: (1) Your contributions to the plan are tax-deductible, much like an IRA contribution. (2) You can pay out-of-pocket medical expenses out of the account, bypassing the need to itemize those expenses on your tax return (which most people won't qualify for anyway). (3) A HSA will enable you to effectively budget for out-of-pocket medical costs, which can often run thousands of dollars at a time and completely disrupt your budget. Much like an IRA, a HSA account can be held in a brokerage account and invested for growth. Those earnings will also accumulate tax free. (4) You can open a HSA with a bank or credit union or, if you expect to invest most or all of your contributions, open an account with a low-cost online broker.

326. **Work your prescriptions.** Get a higher dosage/larger pill and use a pill-cutter to take the right dose. Sometimes this is cheaper.

HOUSING AND RELATED COSTS

327. **Carefully manage your real estate property taxes.** According to a February 25, 2020, post on WalletHub, property taxes cost the average family $2,375 a year. Most people don't know that they can actually contest the property valuation and amount of property taxes and receive a reduction in amounts to be paid. You usually get to do this once per year in most jurisdictions. I have done this successfully for two properties that I have owned. To get the process started, search for the website of your local county assessor, the governmental office that values your property and assesses taxes. Take a look at your valuation and then go to a few real estate sales websites, such as Zillow, and see what the municipality's property tax values are for other homes in your neighborhood. If you believe your home is overvalued, work through the requirements to contest the valuation your home has received.

328. **Begin to compost to provide organic matter for your yard.** You can do this by building a compost bin. This investment will pay off over a few years. If you start tossing your food waste into a compost bin now, though, you won't have to buy tons of fertilizer or expensive soil for your garden next year.

329. **Improve air quality with houseplants.** As an alternative to spending hundreds of dollars on an air purifier, strategically position your houseplants. Plants have long been hailed for their ability remove toxins from the home.

330. **Pay more for the items you use each day.** During my lifetime, I have discovered it is cheaper in the long run to pay extra for certain household items like dishes, knives, storage containers,

furniture and vacuum cleaners. Stepping up a bit in price for quality is worthwhile to get you goods that will last.

331. **Sell or consign your unwanted personal furnishings and clothing.** If you have clothes that are in good condition, consider using a service such as Poshmark, Vinted, Carousell, ThredUp or The RealReal.

332. **Borrow or rent, don't buy, tools needed for one-time projects.** If you need a chainsaw, tree trimmer or power washer for a home project, look to borrow it instead of adding to the pile of once-used tools you have hanging in the garage. Apps like ToolRent or PeerRenters let you get paid for sharing items like drills and cameras within the community.

333. **Rent unused space in your home.** Do you have an extra bedroom, family room over your garage or in-law suite that's not being used? Rent it on a site like Airbnb. Just make sure you know the risks and are willing to take the steps required to protect your family and your possessions.

334. **Cut back on the use of services by doing it yourself.** Due to the pandemic, many of us now have more time at home to take care of maintenance matters. If you hire household services to others, consider cutting back or eliminating them. Instead, put aside some time each week to do them yourself. Not only will you save money, you'll find that many repairs and maintenance activities can get the whole family involved. Using YouTube or Google as resources, you can learn to fix many recurring household repairs and make improvements on your own.

335. **Repair items.** In today's disposable culture, if something is broken, it's sometimes easiest to throw it away and buy a new one. If possible, however, you can repair certain items. Repair that laptop, lamp or lawnmower before reaching into your pocket to buy new. You can check out YouTube tutorials and try to fix it yourself before going to your local repair shop.

336. **Dispose of every household item that doesn't bring you joy.** Marie Kondo has the right idea. I recently downsized my home and can tell you my life is less cluttered with fewer items to maintain. Get rid of the things in your home that you don't use or that you're willing to let go of for the sake of your financial future. That vintage chair your aunt gave you? Sell it. Those music posters you found at the flea market? Sell them. Those boxes in storage that you haven't opened since your last move? Sell the contents. You'd be surprised how much clutter you have in your home. The cash that you can make on those items can be added to your emergency fund.

337. **Don't wait to stop working to downsize your housing.** This is one of the most popular strategies to lower living expenses in retirement, but it works just as well between now and then. After all, housing is typically the single biggest expense most people have. Reducing it in a major way can be the equivalent of minimizing or eliminating 15 or 20 other expenses for housing-related carrying costs.

338. **Get free mulch and wood chips for your flowerbeds.** Sometimes you can get mulch and wood chips for free. Check with your local tree care companies, utility companies and your city. Wood chips reduce weeds but also provide nutrients for your soil.

339. **Improve your home's curb appeal.** Preparing a home for sale or preparing for visiting relatives doesn't have to involve expensive improvement. Clearing the driveway and walkways, trimming the bushes, edging the sidewalk, cleaning the windows to let in natural light and decorating the front with all-season plants may be the most important steps.

340. **Look to sell or rent your parking spot.** If you live in an area where parking can be expensive or hard to come by, consider renting your spot to people when you are not using it. Use this money to save on your own vehicle's expenses and parking. If you no longer have a vehicle, consider selling the parking space for extra cash. Look to web services like Pavemint, SpotHero or Curb-Flip to help you make money from a spot you aren't using.

341. **Plant ground covers in your flowerbeds.** I have used ground covers in my homes over the years to save on buying mulch each year. Ground overs will reduce weeds and add distinction to your yard as they grow and mature. The one-time cost and effort will be much less than if you mulch.

342. **Request a discount on your trash service.** If you are paying for this service, you understand that this can be a highly competitive business. If you get a better offer in the mail for trash service, call your current trash company and ask them to beat the offer.

343. **Take your recycling to the center yourself.** In many communities the cost of recycling is a separate bill each month. Avoid the bill and take your recyclables to the recycling center yourself and save the charge.

344. Save money for a down payment by moving into a family member's basement or spare room. You may be short on savings for that down payment on the home your family needs. If your family is able, moving in with a family member for one or two years can springboard your savings efforts. You will just need to work out the financial and chore-sharing details with your family member. Having multigenerational households has become more common in the US since the pandemic. Properly done, these arrangements can financially and emotionally help all involved.

345. Eliminate private mortgage insurance. For most conventional loans, if the down payment is less than 20%, private mortgage insurance or PMI must be obtained and paid as part of the monthly mortgage payment. Once you have 20% equity in your home, though, you should contact your lender to get your PMI removed. You can build up this equity either by paying down debt or if your home appreciates. Check the terms of the PMI policy to see what actions you need to take if you think you have reached the 20% threshold.

346. Apply for age 65 and older benefits. Many states offer reduced real estate valuations, exemptions, rebates or special rates for individuals over age 65. Be sure to check out what is available in your area and what is involved in filing to obtain the benefits.

347. Apply for tax breaks. Some jurisdictions offer tax breaks for different types of homeowners. You have to ask around or find out to see if you are eligible. Check the website of your state and local governments for details and information on how to apply.

348. **Buy a good quality artificial Christmas tree instead of a new, fresh one each year.** Unless a real tree is a must, you can save money and avoid adding to the post-holiday recycling pile by purchasing a good quality artificial tree. I have done this for the last 20 years and upgrade my tree about every five years, primarily to reduce the cost of Christmas lights. Last year we moved to a tree with LED lights.

349. **Tax breaks for the disabled.** If you are dealing with a disability, investigate if there are special real estate tax exemptions or reductions created especially to help you financially.

350. **Buy a smaller house.** Look to only buy what you use. Carefully assess your space needs, especially now that many of us are working and exercising at home these days. The less space you buy, the more you will save on utilities, real estate taxes, maintenance and holding costs.

351. **Buy your mattress online.** Many sound sleepers have used the growing number of online mattress services to make this important purchase. Sites such as Casper, Leesa, Tuft & Needle and Marpac Yogabed sell high-quality foam mattresses starting around $500. Search for discounts and coupon codes for further savings. There are also inexpensive options on Amazon, but they don't offer the same warranties or trial period.

352. **Check out neighborhood yard, moving and estate sales for tools.** Look for these sales in your community websites and places such as Craigslist. You will be surprised what you can find for very affordable prices.

353. **Consider buying floor-stock/open-box appliances.** Open-box appliances are usually items returned by a customer that are then re-sold at a discount. They come with the manufacturer's warranty and are perfectly fine (sometimes scratched), except they, in some way, did not meet someone else's needs. Similarly, floor stock is also often almost as good as new. As long as you can live with some small imperfections, you're likely to get a significant discount on the item.

354. **Consider using a standing desk.** Standing desks can encourage workers to be less sedentary and offer a nice change from sitting in front of a computer all day. They can save you money on purchasing a desk and can improve your health. Retail prices for desks can reach into the thousands, but there are cheaper solutions, including a wall-mounted shelf or stacking books or boxes to raise the height of a laptop or monitor. Keep feet relaxed by standing on a folded yoga mat or anti-fatigue mat.

355. **Fill your blank walls with objects from your life.** Have an empty wall that's dying for some art but don't have a lot of extra cash? Go through your garage, storage or your kids' old drawings to find interesting pieces to frame. They can help tell the story of your life.

356. **Find a cheaper place to live.** With so many people now working from home permanently you may be able to relocate to a lower cost housing area. If you're renting, move to a less expensive property. If you are a homeowner, look to sell and buy a new lower-priced home in the new location.

357. **Flip or rotate your mattress regularly.** Is your mattress starting to sag or become lumpy? To keep your mattress in good shape and extend its useful life, flip or rotate it a few times per year. (Some mattresses are one-sided and can only be rotated.) Buying a good quality washable mattress cover can help keep your mattress stain free and more hygienic.

358. **Get rid of your storage unit.** Nearly 10% of households rent a self-storage unit. As you move into a home or larger apartment, remember to get your stuff out of storage. Many people hold onto possessions that they don't need and continue to pay that monthly storage cost. Instead, you should think about getting rid of your storage unit as one of the best ways to save money.

359. **It doesn't always pay to buy a home.** Home ownership is part of the American dream and the largest purchase most people make in their lives. You need to be careful buying one before you're financially able. If the housing market in your area is suspect, it can create long-term financial issues for you. Consult a financial professional before you make the leap to home ownership.

360. **Less can be more when it comes to holiday decorations.** At Thanksgiving, for example, it can be tempting to cover every inch of your home with turkey and pumpkin decorations, but less can absolutely be more. It is the thought and consistency of your actions that create the traditions your family will remember. Using family heirlooms and seasonal items that can be reused or eaten can amount to savings over the years.

361. **Make cosmetic changes to a bathroom.** Instead of a major remodel, you may be able to polish the stone, paint the walls,

install new countertops and resurface the tub and shower walls to save money.

362. **Negotiate your rent payment.** Many people think that your rent can't be negotiated. Not true. If there's a rental increase and you've been a good tenant, consider negotiating your rent. Tell your landlord why you've been a good tenant and explain your case. It's expensive for apartment managers to find new tenants. Don't be afraid to attempt to negotiate your rent.

363. **Order bare-root plants online.** These are trees, shrubs, berries and perennials that are sold in a dormant state with no soil on the roots. They are a lot lighter to ship than plants growing in soil and, therefore, less expensive to purchase online. Their light weight makes planting much easier on the back, and the hole you have to dig can be smaller.

364. **Refinance your home loan to lower monthly payments.** Make sure your lender shows you the total interest you'll pay over the entire loan period on the new loan and compare it against the total interest you have left on the current loan. Only go forward if the benefit of lower monthly payments outweighs the potential increase in interest amount.

365. **Reuse common household items.** You may not want to use them forever, but you can reuse disposable items like aluminum foil, Ziplock bags and take-out containers for food storage.

366. **Save money by checking out model home auctions.** After homes in a new development are sold, furnishings in the model homes are often auctioned off at a reduced price. Go to the Builders Auction Company website to find auctions near you.

367. **Save on moving expenses.** You may be able to use one of the truck rental firms to drive your own moving van while hiring people to pack and load/unload for you. This may cost you less than hiring a full-service mover. The best solution depends on your age, the amount and value of your furnishings, if you are being reimbursed for the move and your own willingness to be part of the action.

368. **Set up a regular maintenance schedule for your major appliances and put it on your calendar.** Checking your expensive appliances for dust, leaks or worn out belts will save repair dollars. Cleaning around and under these appliances will keep your home cleaner and your appliances in better working order.

369. **Shop at ReStore.** Habitat for Humanity ReStore locations often have surplus building materials, appliances and used furnishings that are offered at great prices. There are 900 ReStore locations in the US. These locations are benefiting from the Baby Boomer generation's downsizing and offer more and more household items daily. To find one in your area, check habitat.org/restores.

370. **Use the NextDoor app.** Looking for discounted furniture? Free stuff? Gently used moving boxes? Yard tools? Chairs for a party? This app can give you access to all of this. I have used it to find local vendors, repairmen and to sell items I no longer needed.

INCOME TAXES

I could not write this book without including a section on how to save money on your income taxes. I have included a number of general tax tips that apply to most people. As I have stated in all of my books, you should consult a qualified tax professional when adopting a tax strategy or determining how an item should be reported for federal and state income tax purposes.

371. **Maximize your retirement contributions.** Contributing as much as you can to your accounts for your latter years or retirement can create tax benefits for you by reducing your current taxable income. Maximizing contributions to the plans available where you work [e.g., 401(k), 403(b)] is one of the best ways to reap a tax benefit. If you are self employed, you can also make tax-deductible contributions to a Simplified Employee Pension account, or SEP IRA.

372. **Fund a health savings account.** Another way to reduce your taxable income is to contribute to a health savings account (HSA). (You need what is known as a high deductible health plan to do this.) HSAs are also a great way to accumulate assets for when you stop working. The money you put in a HSA has triple tax advantages. The contributions go in pretax, you can withdraw it tax free for qualified medical expenses and any money you do not use can be invested and, as with an IRA or 401(k) plan, the gains are tax deferred.

373. **Collect available tax credits.** There are a significant number of tax credits available that are valuable because they reduce your tax bill on a dollar-for-dollar basis. For example, credits are available to families with children with low or modest incomes (the Earned Income Credit), families can get a credit for each child under age 17 and for parents who use a daycare or childcare service may also be eligible for the federal Child and Dependent Care Tax Credit. Check with your tax advisor to go over the list of

credits, any restrictions on how they can be claimed and which ones are available to you.

374. **Research for available deductions.** Work with your tax advisor to look for all deductions you are entitled to including mortgage interest, real estate and property taxes and medical expenses to see if you have enough to itemize your deductions. The Tax Cuts and Jobs Act raised the bar on who will itemize, as you now must surpass the 2021 standard deductions of $12,550 for singles or $25,100 for a married couple filing jointly

375. **Invest in municipal bonds.** Buying a municipal bond essentially means lending money to a state or local entity for a set number of interest payments over a predetermined period. Interest earned on municipal bonds is exempt from federal taxes and may be tax exempt at the state and local level as well depending on where you live.

376. **Plan for long-term capital gains.** Investing can be an important tool in growing wealth. An additional benefit from investing in stocks, mutual funds, bonds and real estate is the favorable tax treatment for long-term capital gains. An investor holding an asset for longer than one year enjoys a preferential tax rate of 0%, 15% or 20% on the capital gain, depending on your income level. If the asset is held for less than a year before selling, the capital gain is taxed at ordinary income rates.

377. **Establish an IRA.** Individual Retirement Accounts are a straight-forward, easily accessible way to cut your taxes the same way the 401(k) does, but they have strict rules. If neither you nor your spouse participate in a workplace retirement plan, then for 2021 you can contribute $6,000 ($7,000 if you're 50 or older) to an IRA

and take that off your taxable income—even if you don't itemize deductions.

378. **Plan your charitable contributions.** If you plan to make a significant deductible gift to charity, consider giving appreciated stocks or mutual fund shares that you've owned for more than one year instead of cash. Your charitable contribution deduction is the fair market value of the securities on the date of the gift, not the amount you paid for the asset, and you never have to pay tax on the profit. However, don't donate stocks for fund shares that lost money. You'd be better off selling the asset, claiming the loss on your taxes and then donating the cash proceeds to the charity.

379. **Keep track of your costs of supporting charities.** Add up all out-of-pocket costs of doing good. Keep track of what you spend while doing charitable work, from what you spend on stamps for a fundraiser, to the cost of ingredients for casseroles you make for the homeless and be sure to track the number of miles you drive your care for charity. Add such costs with your cash contributions when figuring your charitable contribution deduction.

380. **Your residential energy saving expenditures may be tax friendly.** A tax credit is available for homeowners who install alternative energy equipment. It equals a percentage of what a homeowner spends on qualifying property such as solar electric systems, solar hot water heaters, geothermal heat pumps and wind turbines, including labor costs. There is a cap on this tax credit of 26% in 2020 and 22% in 2021.

381. **Caregiving expenses may have tax benefits.** After taxes it can easily take $7,500 or more of salary to pay $5,000 worth of child-care expenses. If you use a childcare reimbursement account at

work to pay those bills, you get to use pre-tax dollars. That can save you one-third or more of the cost since you avoid both income and Social Security taxes. The maximum you can set aside tax free is $5,000. If your boss offers such a plan, take advantage of it. This isn't just for children. If you have a spouse or relative who is physically or mentally incapable of self care and lives in your home, they're eligible too. The tax law also expands to allow Achieving a Better Life Experience (ABLE) accounts, which permits families to put aside up to $15,000 a year to cover expenses for a beneficiary with special needs.

382. **Look carefully at the availability of your work tuition reimbursement plans.** Companies can offer employees up to $5,250 of educational assistance tax free each year. This amount is not taxable to you and is treated as a tax-free fringe benefit. It could really help you pay to improve your knowledge and skills.

INSURANCE

383. **Understand the financial cost of the risks you should insure against.** There are certain financial risks each person must identify, eliminate or minimize in their lifetime. An individual needs to understand the risks they are facing (e.g., premature death, health, disability, longevity) and what they can do to deal with each situation. Insurance can provide a cost-effective solution to protect against these risks.

384. **Drop vehicle collision coverage on older models.** The Insurance Information Institute suggests that comprehensive and collision coverage doesn't make sense when a car's

value is ten times or less of its annual cost to purchase colli-sion coverage. This move could save you a good chunk of change.

385. **Buy renters insurance to protect your possessions.** You should always buy renters insurance even if you don't have many pos-sessions. Renters insurance covers theft of personal property even if it occurs outside the home and, most importantly, lia-bility protection in the event someone is injured and sues. If that major fire or storm hits your area, having this coverage could pay off for you.

386. **Look for discounts on when and how you pay your premi-ums.** Many times insurance companies will offer discounts if you pay your premiums by bank account auto-pay or if you just pay semi-annually or annually. You may be surprised on what you save.

387. **Understand the income tax advantages of life insurance.** Life insurance has been designed, and Congress has bestowed upon it, the ability to provide tax-free death benefits to beneficiaries, tax-deferred accumulation and tax-free access to cash value using loans or withdrawals. Most consumers do not understand these advantages nor do they use them to their advantage.

388. **Look to raise the deductibles or coinsurance amounts for all of your coverages.** You could be paying large premiums in order to have small deductibles and could save dollars by increasing those amounts. Raising your deductible or coinsurance amounts can often significantly reduce your annual premiums, easing the monthly strain on your bills. Just be sure you have the funds in your emergency fund to pay the amounts.

389. **Life insurance can generate cash accumulation and savings.** Permanent policies (not term insurance) are designed to build cash value, like whole life and universal life. These forms of permanent life insurance give the owner access to cash by being surrendered, loaned against or having cash withdrawn before the insured person passes away. The key for the consumer is that the cash value taken from the policy is not restricted and can be used for any purpose, including funding college costs, funding wedding costs, supplementing retirement income, starting a business or fulfilling another personal need.

390. **Bundle your coverages with one insurance company.** Most insurance companies will offer you a significant (i.e., 5% or more) discount for having multiple policies with them. This is called bundling your policies. Consider this when you place your coverage with a carrier.

391. **Audit your own driving habits and mileage.** Have you recently moved out of an urban area? Did you just switch jobs? Are you working from home? Given how our lives have changed with the pandemic, you might be surprised with the savings you will find. In particular, know how many miles you drive each year. Driving less will reduce your car insurance rates because the less you drive, obviously, the less chance you have of getting into an accident. The premiums should be much lower.

392. **Select a lower-grade (higher out-of-pocket) health insurance plan.** Understand the deductibles, coinsurance and monthly costs for your coverage and make choices that make economic sense. Overall, I look at what my total out-of-pocket cost would be for each option and make my selection based on that. If you

don't have enough in your emergency fund to cover higher out-of-pocket medical costs, you should probably stick to those plans that give you the most coverage.

393. **Look into disability insurance.** You need to protect yourself against the loss of employment income and premature death. Without an income you cannot save or provide for your household. A basic concept in financial planning is to protect against your downside risks. For most people, the main risks are the loss of their income or life. Protections for these risks can be purchased today at the most affordable rates in decades with life insurance and disability income products.

394. **Shop for your homeowners insurance and auto insurance at least every two years.** You can save money and possibly improve the coverage you have by shopping around. If you haven't had losses, have a great driving record or if your credit score is strong or much improved, you might be able to save money spent on premiums.

395. **Tell your insurer about your home upgrades.** Stay in touch with your general insurance agent or company about changes in your home. If you installed smoke detectors, a new monitored alarm system or new impact-resistant windows in a hurricane prone area, your insurance company might discount your premiums. Check with the Insurance Information Institute for information and ideas on which improvements can save you premium dollars and generate the most discounts.

396. **Think twice before submitting an insurance claim**. My rule of thumb is that I won't submit a claim on a loss that is less than

twice my deductible. So, for a $500 deductible on an auto loss, I'll pay out of pocket any loss up to $1,000. Why? The $500 I'd receive from my insurance company is not worth the increased premiums I'm likely to pay. You may want to call your insurance agent to find out how a claim will impact your premiums before filing the claim.

397. **Avoid being unconsciously over insured.** Some consumers want to reduce their exposure to risk to the maximum extent they can. You should only buy the insurance coverage you need for your financial situation. Work with an insurance professional to make sure you are properly covered but not over covered.

398. **Get the discounts available for your teenage drivers.** Young drivers almost always pay more for coverage, but sometimes you can get substantial discounts if your teen maintains good grades, takes a behind-the-wheel driving course or completes mandated online classes.

399. **Have all of your teenagers use the same car.** You can usually save money if you have your new drivers use the same (hopefully your safest and oldest) least-expensive vehicle.

400. **If you directly pay for your own health insurance, do an annual coverage and price check.** Perform a full search on your state's health insurance exchange or use one of the available apps such as eHealth. Whether you currently have health insurance or you're thinking of applying for it, it's always a great idea to shop around to make sure you're getting the best deal.

401. **Ask for discounts to lower your auto insurance premiums.** There are many ways to get discounts on your policy,

including taking a defensive driving class, installing an anti-theft device or installing a safe-driving device. Asking for available discounts could save you money.

402. **Choose a replacement cost policy.** When you buy homeowners and renters policies, elect replacement cost coverage that pays if you have a loss. This will ensure you receive the newest model of an item if it needs to be replaced.

403. **Discuss changes in your life with your insurance provider at least annually.** Be sure to review your insurance coverages after life events such as getting married, having/adopting a child, changing jobs or using your vehicle for a side gig. You need to make sure your coverage is appropriate for your changed life circumstances.

404. **See if you qualify for group insurance coverage.** For example, accountants who are CPAs may be able to get discounted life, home and personal liability coverages through the American Institute of Certified Public Accountants.

INVESTMENTS

405. **Look to maximize any matched contributions your employer offers for retirement savings.** One of the great parts of investing through a 401(k) is that the money you put in isn't taxed until you withdraw it. At that point, it's likely that you'll be in a lower tax bracket because your income will be less than it was when you originally earned the money. However, one of the best perks of a 401(k) is that your employer may offer to match a portion of your 401(k) contributions. (The average match is around 3%.) This is

free money and you'd be crazy not to take advantage of this as much as possible. You should do everything you can to max out your 401(k) to get all of your employer's matched contributions.

406. Buy low or no-cost mutual funds. Fund fees have a major impact on investment returns. Carefully consider whether lower cost funds meet your needs for growth and cost management. Sometimes paying additional fees for active investment management can pay for itself. Just be aware of what you are paying for investment management.

407. Start investing if you can. This may not seem like the most obvious of the tips in a book of money-saving tips, but it is something you need to think about and act on. Investing means you will have to put some of your money out there to start earning more in your savings. Investing is easier these days, and you can begin with very little cash once you have accumulated money in your emergency fund and have either paid off or substantially reduced your debts.

408. Don't procrastinate in planning for your later years. Many folks hold off on planning for retirement. This mindset is common among people at all economic levels. Unless they are about to experience something—they treat it as out of sight out of mind. They assume that there will be a more opportune time to start planning for their financial future. This may be because their anticipated cash flow will improve when their kids are out of the house, they will be earning more money after a promotion at work or they will experience a meaningful liquidity event after the sale of their business. In reality, the longer one waits, the harder it is to save and accumulate wealth. There is no better time to start saving than the present.

409. **Carefully plan for your Fulfilling Stage.** Once you have funded your household's emergency fund, you need to begin plan your savings for the long-term or Fulfilling Stage of your life. An individual retirement account or IRA is a pooled retirement investment managed by financial professionals. The government allows you to contribute to your IRA annually, so make sure you are maximizing your contributions. Using an IRA or mutual fund, a money manager invests on your behalf in the stock and bond markets. These individuals have expertise in finding high-yielding assets that offer low risk. The power of compounding interest makes this an ideal financial vehicle for long-term savings for the family.

410. **Understand the impact of investment fees.** Access FINRA's fund analyzer to better understand what you are paying and how it impacts your returns. Visit finra.org to check the fees in your mutual funds and compare the costs. One of the biggest money wasters when investing is the fees that are often charged to manage your money. These can really eat into your returns over time to the tune of tens of thousands of dollars. You should understand what you are paying and do the research to see if the fees charged are too much.

411. **Buy slices or fractional shares of stock.** Stocks like Amazon and Tesla go for large amounts per share but brokerage firms, such as Fidelity, now let you buy fractional shares or slices. You can purchase small amounts and build positions in the stocks you love but can't afford full-share prices.

412. **Invest with a low-cost online broker.** If you are managing your own investments, consider using one of the online brokers to do your investment trading, as many have gone the no commission route. Avoid the expensive broker that charges you an arm and a leg each time you trade.

PETS

413. **Think before you bring home a pet.** I'm not saying get rid of your cat or dog (adoptions have risen during the pandemic) but, if you're thinking about adopting a pet, hold off until you're out of debt. They can be very expensive. Adopting a pet from an animal shelter costs $50 to $100, and that's just the beginning. Between food and veterinarian care, you're looking at over $500 a year— and that's if you don't indulge them. If you want to treat your dog or cat like you'd want to be treated, you'll need to throw in toys, flea-and-tick treatments, grooming and a comfortable bed. That can add up to over $1,500 a year. If you want to treat your pet well, you'll also spend money for stuff like teeth cleaning, professional training, boarding when you travel and possibly high medical costs as the pet ages.

414. **Adopt the right type and breed.** Considering a new pet? Experts say purebred cats and dogs are most prone to illness— and the accompanying vet bills. In general, the pets that cost the least to care for are small, female mixed breeds that have been spayed.

415. **Buy pet supplies in bulk.** Pets can be expensive. If you know you need items like cat litter or cat food, why not buy in bulk? You can

score some additional savings by buying your must-have items in bulk at pet-focused websites and wholesale clubs like Costco.

416. **Shop for a reasonably priced veterinarian.** To save on out-of-pocket costs for pet medical bills, shop around before choosing a vet. Look for discount packages and focus on preventive care. Remember, carefully looking after your pet's needs for diet, exercise and regular check-ups will keep the animal healthier and save you money.

SAVINGS ACCOUNTS

417. **Save a set percentage of your paycheck.** If you have a full-time job where your employer is already withholding taxes, you should still aim to put away something each payday. (Some people target 10% to 20% of the paycheck; but, depending on your situation, that can be impossible.) Try to settle on an amount you're comfortable with, no matter how small. If you're a freelancer, look to save a percentage of your gross profits each month.

418. **Set up a separate bank account with a bank other than your main bank.** Deposit any extra money windfalls you get in that account whenever possible. This will create a nice barrier between you and your savings. Of all of the ways to save money, this may be one of the most effective.

419. **Move your savings to a high interest online savings account.** Even in this low interest rate world, you can increase the amount of interest income you receive by 5 times or more. If you're like most people, you probably have your savings stashed in a local bank. If so, your interest rate is likely quite low. If you look at the

national interest rate of about .1 % at the time this book was written, your savings won't experience much growth. Banks know the primary reason people open an account is because there's a bank branch nearby. You can do a lot better by going against the grain and finding an online bank that pays a much higher rate. That's really where you need to store your savings.

420. **Set yourself up to save automatically.** If you have to manually transfer money into your accounts, you may be more likely to forgo saving altogether. Try having a portion of your paycheck automatically deposited into a savings account to keep you contributing consistently. Also, only use the savings account for designated purposes, such as funds for your emergency fund, a house purchase or dream vacation.

421. **Open a certificate of deposit.** Once you have accumulated more than $10,000 in your emergency fund, you should look to put the money into a higher earning online certificate of deposit through your Internet bank. This will grow your savings faster than the savings accounts.

422. **Open a money market account.** In some situations, opening a money market account can increase the amount of interest you earn.

SIDE GIGS

423. **Sell your hobby creations to earn extra cash.** Make your entertainment time earn you money as well. If there's a hobby or skill you do for fun, consider selling the fruits of your labor. If you love

photography, try selling photos on stock websites. If you find yourself writing at the end of the day, try starting a blog.

424. **Become a virtual assistant to earn money online.** Virtual assistant tasks may include social media management, formatting and editing content, scheduling appointments or travel, email management and more. Basically, you can get paid to do any task that needs to be done in someone's business but doesn't need to be done by them. Learn more at makingsenseofcents.com.

425. **Sell on Amazon.** Become a reseller on Amazon. Many individuals have found that they can buy low and sell higher by becoming a reseller. If you are looking for a retail side gig, this may be a lucrative option to consider.

426. **Become a pet sitter.** If you're an animal lover, getting paid to play with other people's animals could be an excellent option for you and help you save additional money. Depending on the owners' needs, you may even be able to keep their pet at your home, making it more convenient work for you. Apps like Rover make it easy to connect with owners.

427. **Teach English online to earn money at home.** Work from home, create your own schedule and earn $18-$21 per hour (many teachers are earning over $1,000 per month) while teaching English online. To learn more, visit makingsenseofcents.com.

428. **Become a flea market flipper.** Start this gig by keeping an eye out for things that could be flipped when thrift shopping. If you go shopping at thrift stores to save money, you can also use this time to keep an eye out for things that would be good to resell (or

"flip") to get some extra cash. There is even a television show that demonstrates how financially rewarding this activity can be.

429. **Start a blog.** This isn't a way to cut expenses, but there are many ways that a blog can help you save more money. A blog can encourage you to keep track of your finances, introduce you to others interested in saving more and help you make extra money. I know many people who have started a blog and are making a reasonable income every month.

430. **Take as many online surveys as you can.** There are tons of survey companies that you can sign up for and make a little bit of side cash. If you sign up for all of them, you may be able to earn anywhere from $25-$100+ a month by taking surveys online. Survey companies making this available include makingsenseofcents.com/swagbucks, makingsenseofcents.com/surveyjunkie and harrispollonline.com. They're free to join and free to use! You get paid to answer surveys and to test products. It's best to sign up for as many as you can. That way, you can receive the most surveys and make the most money.

431. **Take on a work-from-home side gig to increase your household income.** By applying for a second job, you get to bring in more money for the family. Unfortunately, trading your time for cash can also take a toll on your family life as well. Kids need parents around while they are growing up. If the parents are both at work all day and night, then there's little room left for developing family relationships. On the other hand, financial hardship can cause parents to pay more attention to the bills than they do the kids. With the advent of the Internet, anyone can make more money from the comfort of home.

432. **Test websites and get paid.** Website developers always need people to check that their site works well and is user friendly. There is now a company that will pay you to do just that! The website TestingTime will pay you for each 20-minute test. All you need is a computer with a webcam and a microphone.

SPENDING HABITS

433. **Adopt a savings mindset.** One of the biggest challenges in personal finance is figuring out ways to spend less money. One of the best ways to accomplish that is to adopt the mindset of reducing your monthly expenses. Even though some of our regular bills might seem small and insignificant on their own, their cumulative effect can be enormous and become a huge drain on our resources. Always look for savings and you will find them.

434. **Know when to ask for help with your financial situation.** You must learn who you can reach out to in order to solve financial problems. Get to know bankers, financial planners, insurance professionals, investment professionals and, if necessary, legal resources to get your issues addressed and resolved. There are different types of qualified people that can help get you the answers you need.

435. **Understand the terms of your bills.** It is a great idea to complete a thorough review of all of your monthly bills. Study the fine print to see exactly what you are being charged and why. For example, you may save if you pay a bill on an annual basis versus a monthly basis. Also, stop any charges for services you aren't using.

436. **Ride the adaptation phenomenon wave. There is** a psychological phenomenon known as "adaptation." This means that when something happens—positive or negative—you soon get used to it and return to feeling like your "old self." (If it does not kill you, it will make you stronger.) For instance, if you get a raise, you'll initially enjoy the extra cash to spend but will soon become accustomed to your new budget and accept it as the new normal. The other side of the coin is that we adjust to disappointments in the same way. Luckily, resetting your expectations may not be as difficult as you thought. Plus, if saving more is important to you, then you really want to make this a long-term habit.

437. **Buy online when it saves you money**. Amazon offers "Subscribe and Save" services that can save you money on buying everyday essentials on a recurring basis. For example, I use this for my orders of protein bars and vitamins.

438. **Always ask for a discount.** Whenever you can, don't be afraid to ask for a discount. The worst they can say is no. Next time you're getting tickets at a movie theater, museum or sporting event, check to see if they have any special discounts for seniors, students, teachers, military or AAA members.

439. **Avoid watching commercials.** This is one of my extreme ideas. Whether you realize it or not, you are constantly being exposed to advertisements throughout the day. Don't make this worse by spending your time watching commercials or clicking on Internet ads that can have a negative impact on your spending habits. These ads are all designed by very clever people to get your attention and call you to action. The fewer ads you see and fewer links you click, the less likely you will be influenced to spend.

440. **Understand how you can buy things.** There are five major ways you can pay for the things, products and services that you need. Understanding this can be beneficial and help you make your cash go further. These include buying, renting, bartering, subscribing and getting them for free in exchange for your personal data. So, which of the five ways is best? You will not like my answer—as it depends. Renting a house may provide the best economic outcome for you. You may, however, feel more psychologically secure owning your own home and having exclusive use and control of it. The key is knowing that there are different ways to get the use of an asset, product or service and choosing the way that is best for you at that particular time.

441. **Buy only what you need, just enough of what you need and only when you need it.**

442. **Buy used or get free items.** When you are making a purchase, check eBay, Craigslist, Facebook Marketplace or your local thrift stores to see if you can find a used item for free or much less. You might even find that people are giving the item away. This happens a lot when people move or downsize.

443. **Do not buy things from vending machines.** You may be paying a large premium for the convenience offered.

444. **Return broken or poor quality purchases.** Fully leverage the return policy for products that you ended up not using or products that don't fulfill their promise or intended use. Please don't abuse the company's policy, as you may be tagged as someone who does this. Remember, it is okay to return a product that does not perform as advertised.

445. **Stop spending for one weekend.** This is a practice recommended by many money savers. It is a two-day course of action that could lead to a lifetime of savings. Try to go an entire Saturday and Sunday without buying anything. Eat what's already in your refrigerator or pantry. Drink what's in the liquor cabinet. Instead of going to a movie, watch one on TV, read a book, take your kids to a park or play board games with your family. Not only will you save money, you might discover some of the better things in life really are free.

446. **Take a mindfulness break before making a purchase.** Wait before you buy it. Wait at least 24 hours (some experts say a 30-day waiting period is ideal) before you buy something that's not essential. This way, you will have time to avoid an impulse buy.

447. **Use what you have until it is worn out.** Don't prematurely replace items just because there is something newer available. Your two model ago cell phone will likely serve you just fine.

448. **Always consider the trade-off.** Think about saving money in terms of trade-offs—save money here, spend it there. If you're planning on a vacation this year, keep that in mind as you are looking to save money elsewhere. It'll give you a sense of accomplishment as you save more towards a particular goal and will motivate you to be more creative

449. **Take baby steps with your savings actions but think big long term.** The truth is, people are more successful when they set and complete a series of short-term goals (think the Snowball Method of repaying debt). For instance, committing to saving $15 a week

on groceries or $30 a month on gas for the car can add up over time.

450. **Be less of a consumer and limit the amount of stuff you have.** I recently downsized and moved, and I cannot tell you how many times my wife and I repeatedly asked ourselves "Why did we buy all of this stuff?" It caused us to rethink our spending habits. Today, we ask ourselves if we really need the item or if we can live without it. As a result, our spending on discretionary items has decreased substantially.

451. **Calculate the cost of purchases by hours you have to work to pay for them.** This tactic really helps you to better psychologically frame what you are spending. Take the amount of the item you want to purchase and divide it by your hourly wage. For example, if you're considering a $50 pair of shoes and you make $15 an hour, ask yourself if those shoes are worth working for four hours. Sometimes they are, sometimes they won't be.

452. **Check your product and service warranties and use them for repairs.** If something breaks, as things inevitably do, don't immediately run out to buy a replacement. Look to utilize any available warranties or free repair offers you can find. Some manufacturers are so proud of their products that they will repair them for free. All of my warranties are safely kept in a file. After opening the packaging of a product be sure to hold on to any warranty information provided.

453. **Clean out your home at least once per year—you might find exactly what you need.** This is coming from someone who recently found several summer shirts that I bought and put in a drawer for safekeeping. This hoard was discovered shortly

attempting to put away a new purchase. Luckily, I was able to return that new purchase.

454. **Delete your credit card information from online accounts.** Make it difficult to buy impulsively from websites by deleting your credit card information from their system. This will force you to take time to consider your purchase as you type in your number.

455. **Do your shopping where there's competition.** Where farmers' markets are back in business, remember that lots of vendors will have produce that's being harvested locally—so the price will be lowest for those items. Skip the shopping list in this case. Buy what's abundant, freeze excess food items purchased and choose recipes based on what you buy.

456. **Don't keep large amounts of cash in your pocket.** Do not carry a lot of money with you when you go out. So even if you are tempted to buy something, you won't. If you really need to buy the item, you will have to return home for the money. If the item is not needed, then you just saved yourself the trip home and the spend.

457. **Don't overspend on personal hygiene products.** I know this can be a sensitive subject but just read ahead. Most people would probably find that off-brand or lower-priced products work just as well as the more costly options. The key is to use this stuff regularly and consistently. There is no need to buy that special $40 shampoo or $35 hair gel.

458. **Don't be a passive consumer.** Prepare in advance when you might be stuck in a place where the pricing is marked up because

of low competition (e.g. movie theater, sports venue, zoo, etc.). Bring your own snack or eat at home just before heading to these places.

459. **Fully use all the cosmetics and cleaning supplies you buy.** *Yes, I am talking about that annoying habit of making sure you get the last drop of laundry detergent, fabric softener and toothpaste from the tube. You would be surprised how much you can save on these expensive items.*

460. **Keep all of your gift cards in one place so you don't misplace them.** It's easy to lose track of gift cards. Try to keep them all in one place where you can look through them every time you plan to make a purchase.

461. **Live below your means.** This is the easiest idea for me to write about but probably the hardest for people to implement. We live in a competitive and consumer-driven US economy. Making a conscious decision not to buy things that other people already have is really hard to do. The problem arises when you are trying to "keep up with the Joneses," leading you to spend money you do not have. You might put expenses on credit cards to "afford" things. You might also buy things that you do not care about. This can lead to an excessive amount of debt and potentially set you back years with your financial goals. In reality, you should spend your money as you see fit to satisfy your needs. Overspending in order to keep up with others can have a disastrous effect on your financial life.

462. **Look at Internet reviews before you buy.** Do your research before you buy an expensive item or service (e.g., doctors, dentists, hair stylists). Check reviews on Amazon, look up reviews

online, check a few forums or look up prices at different stores. I have found these reviews to be helpful and valuable.

463. **Negotiate, negotiate, negotiate.** It's often possible to negotiate lower costs for different services. Not everyone is comfortable with going through the negotiation process, especially with service providers whose personnel are programmed to say "no." Well, don't worry there is an app called Recoup that will handle the negotiations for you. They can help you lower costs for banking, credit cards and subscriptions from providers and merchants. All you need do is connect your service providers to the app and Recoup will get to work. That'll make the whole job of negotiating easier on you.

464. **Reduce personal grooming expenses.** If there is one thing we all learned during the pandemic, to the detriment of the hair and beauty industry, is that we could stretch the length of time between haircuts and hair colors. Instead of having our hair cut and styled monthly, we can add another few weeks between appointments. If you have your nails done twice a month, try it once a month. If you buy expensive shampoos, look at lower cost options. Bottomline—we have learned that exposing our gray hair for a short span of time is now accepted by everyone.

465. **Restrain yourself from making unnecessary purchases.** Avoid buying things you will only use once, such as formal wear (rent instead), specialty kitchen appliances (which lose their novelty quickly) and power tools (rent from home improvement stores or borrow from local sources).

466. **Saving money begets saving money.** Once you start finding ways to save money (and watching your bank account grow), it

will start to become a good financial habit. It's a mindset shift that allows you to reevaluate certain practices and habits in your life to benefit your future financial security.

467. **Trade services with a neighbor.** While not monetary income, you can earn favors by trading jobs with your neighbors or friends. For example, you can take turns babysitting your friend's kids or watch your neighbor's pets while they're out in exchange for them mowing your lawn.

468. **Visit thrift stores.** Thrift store buys can provide great value, and they will be a lot cheaper. Stores like Goodwill and local thrift stores are great for finding clothing for children and adults, home décor and household goods like dishes and flatware. You can surprise yourself with your finds and the low prices you will pay.

469. **Add a virtual change bucket.** Apps like Qapital and Acorns round up your purchases to the nearest dollar and add the difference into an investment account. Users can direct those extra pennies toward a savings account.

470. **Buy only what babies actually need.** This idea is one I only began to practice with the birth of my third child. I should have done it sooner. Stores and parenting blogs are full of recommendations of what you should buy for your newborn. Before buying everything on their lists, consider shopping with a friend who's already a parent. They'll be able to tell you what you'll actually need to support your newborn—not what the stores want to sell you.

471. **Complete a no-spend challenge.** No spending challenges are a great way to improve your awareness of just what you are spending your precious money on. You can take this challenge for a day,

week, month or any period you choose that you can complete. A no-spend challenge is a drastic challenge to help you reset your daily spending habits to realize what truly brings you value and what you can live without.

472. **Confirm it's really a sale price before you buy.** If you aren't sure whether a price is good, plug it into a free price tracking, such as the Wikibuy, CamelCamelCamel or Pricepulse, to check.

473. **Don't buy lottery tickets or gamble at the casino.** Gambling at the casino and playing the lottery are both risky moves, and you are spending your money with little odds of a successful return. In the US alone, people lose over $100 billion gambling each year (that doesn't even include money lost playing the lottery). According to Bloomberg, the average person who plays the lottery in the US not only spends around $300 a year on lottery tickets, they also lose approximately $0.40 for every $1 in tickets purchased. Overall, the odds of losing outweigh the odds of winning. You will likely be much better off if you steer clear of gambling.

474. **Find a cash savings buddy.** If you are single, you might need a partner to keep you on track for your savings journey. Find a friend to embark on this savings journey with you and meet to discuss your progress and results. This accountability will reinforce good habits. Having a partner should also help you stick to your savings plans.

475. **Get motivated about saving money.** Find a passion for saving money. Not because you want to hoard all of your cash, but because you want to use it for good. Think about how many lives you could change if you saved more of your money for

worthwhile donations. Think about how great your kid's future could be if you saved more money for their education and general well-being. And don't forget about your own retirement. Enjoy watching your savings grow knowing that you won't have to depend on someone else in the future.

476. **Go on a cash diet.** Put your credit card in the drawer and only use cash for your purchases. Cash only purchases will ensure you spend only what you have on hand. This can help you save money and avoid debt. Know your spending triggers or why you buy. We all have spending triggers—stress, relationship issues or the need to keep up with our friends. Spending triggers can be certain emotions that encourage you to spend. If you indulge in retail therapy after a bad day, that's a trigger. Knowing your spending triggers can help you avoid spending when you don't need to.

477. **Organize a neighborhood swap meet.** Here's how it works. Gather your friends and neighbors with kids around the same age and everyone brings gently used clothing, books, school supplies, toys, etc. Each person receives a ticket for each item they bring. Each ticket entitles you to one item from the swap meet. If you contribute six books, you can leave with up to six new-to-you books. If you contribute seven items of clothing, you can leave with up to seven new-to-you items of clothing. All leftover items are donated.

478. **Review your bills for errors.** Mistakes happen. Unfortunately, the bank rarely deposits an extra $10,000 into your account in error. Most mistakes are usually innocent and are easy to fix as long as you take the time to contact the company involved.

Correcting the errors may also help you from having improper information reported to the credit bureaus.

479. **Sell unused items.** Dig through your closets or attic and look for items you no longer use that may have value, then sell them through consignment, eBay or Craigslist. You can then use the money you bring in to pay off debt and put it behind you once and for all.

480. **Shop at stores with liberal return policies.** Although many stores have tightened their return policies, look for ones that have a more consumer-friendly policy. Nordstrom is a longtime favorite, and there are several other stores with similar approaches, including Costco.

481. **Shop online first, in the store second.** One of the smartest ways to save money is to always comparison shop online before going to actual stores. Consider using Wikibuy to save you money before you spend by helping you find lower prices. This will allow you to find the best deal without wasting time and gas driving around town. It will also assure you that you will get the model or specific merchandise you are looking for.

482. **Make a major philosophical change and simplify your life by becoming a minimalist.** Trying to manage your life, especially your financial life, can be difficult today. Between learning about money saving tips, planning for retirement, paying bills, raising a family, etc., life can be exhausting. By adopting a minimalist lifestyle you can learn how to be happier, have more control over your life and waste less of your valuable time and money. Simplifying your life can include learning to be more organized, developing good money habits, becoming

debt free, de-cluttering your living space and spending money mindfully. There are a number of books and websites you can research to find out more on this subject.

483.   **Try to eliminate one service each year that you can do without.** Take a critical look at all the services you pay for and decide to do without one each year. From having your nails done to getting your dog groomed, there are savings to be found. It may only save you $25 to $50 per month, but over the years it really adds up.

484.   **Use cash for better negotiations.** Larger ticket items definitely benefit from you waving around cash. You're able to negotiate great deals when they see you're a serious buyer. I was able to save $100 on a recent house repair by paying cash on the spot.

485.   **Always invest in quality.** Think about spending a bit more money on things that will last longer. For example, it can be worth it to buy higher quality clothing (as long as they're not for young children) because you won't have to replace them as often. You will be surprised how long quality can last if you take good care of it.

486.   **Use the 24-hour rule for purchases less than $100.** This is similar to the 30-day rule, but for less expensive purchases. Wait a day before buying a small item and you may find you didn't want it after all.

487.   **Stop collecting things and sell what you have accumulated.** There was a time when people thought their collections of dolls, toys and china figurines would bring them riches down the road when it was time to sell them as antiques. Beanie Babies and Cabbage Patch Kids were big fads at one time. Now, with the advent of technology, you can find most of these items on resale

sites like eBay, at flea markets and at garage sales for a fraction of their initial cost. Many people, who sunk thousands of dollars into their collectibles, now realize their worth to be only a few dollars. To avoid this situation, don't collect items of questionable value. If you want to recoup some of the money you've already spent, start selling your collectibles now and use those funds for any number of worthy financial goals.

488. **Use a simple razor to shave.** I've used the same brand for a long time and avoided upgrading to the available, more expensive models. I shave in the shower and dry off the blade afterwards. There has been much competition in the shaving space in the last few years, and you should be able to find a cost-effective razor that will not require you to surrender an arm and a leg to purchase.

489. **Limit your spending with an allowance.** It's fine to spend some money on random indulgences, but you can keep it from getting out of hand by using an allowance system where you get a certain amount of money to spend on a weekly or monthly basis. I have always taken 1% of any source of unexpected cash and used it for the extravagant items I wanted to buy.

SUBSCRIPTIONS

490. **Cancel all print newspaper and magazine subscriptions.** You are joining the crowd if you take this action. I recently cancelled all of my print magazine subscriptions and moved to a combined digital subscription from Apple that gives me access to all of my favorite magazines for much less than I was paying for individual

subscriptions. I also like this because I no longer have any issues with address changes or vacation periods. When I go away, I no longer come back to a stack of magazines that require recycling.

491. **Cut or reduce unneeded or unused subscription services like credit monitoring, gym memberships, associations, etc.** Saving on recurring expenses means that you will enjoy the savings every month going forward.

492. **Always sign up for automatic payments or autopay.** You can normally save on many of your bills by setting up payments this way. For cell phone and cable service you can save —$5 to $10 per line—on eligible plans for customers who use automatic payments. That can add up to significant savings, especially if you have a family plan with several lines.

493. **Reduce your subscriptions using a service.** One such app is AskTrim.

TECHNOLOGY

494. **Bundle your technology.** Sometimes you can save by bundling your TV, Internet and phone services. This can typically save you good money each month. Again, be careful and purchase only the services you use.

495. **Call and ask your carrier if you can get a better deal.** Ask about specials being offered to new customers and if they have any retention offers for existing customers about to switch.

496. **Check to see if your employer or any of the associations or groups you belong to offer cell phone discounts.** You may be

able to get lower prices based on your age or affiliation with certain groups. Carriers also commonly offer price breaks to military members, first responders or educators. Membership with an association such as AARP or AAA may also score you deals. All of the major carriers offer dedicated plans for seniors.

497. **Cut back on your cable service plan.** If you don't want to eliminate cable completely and become a cord cutter, look to pare down your plan. If you must have cable, take a look at all of the charges on your cable bill and consider getting rid of some of the services. Try it for a month and see if you really miss those last 500 channels.

498. **Don't take the device insurance plan if you normally treat your phone very well and are not someone who often loses your phone.** When you sign up for a wireless plan and buy a phone, you'll likely be offered insurance in case your device is damaged, lost or stolen. For those of you who are accident-prone, insurance may be worthwhile, especially for a pricey device. Otherwise, simply using a protective case, which helps shield your device from everyday bangs and bumps, may be enough to get by. You can set aside the money you would have spent on insurance premiums—often about $10 to $20 per month—for backup in case you need to repair or replace your phone at some point. If you normally handle your device with care, you'll likely save money.

499. **Buy a used device.** This is a great way to buy not only computers but smartphones as well. You can check out the details on how to buy refurbished devices by making a quick Google search. This can save you a great deal. Just be sure you're getting the product from a reputable company. Keep in mind, like most used items, a

pre-owned phone may come with a few cosmetic bumps, bruises and scratches.

500. **If your phone is not the most important thing to you, consider getting a less costly model.** With the improvements in technology, the lower-priced offerings may provide the key functionality you need and use for less expense.

501. **Look to use open-source software when possible**. Many people use the free application GIMP instead of Photoshop.

502. **Make sure all of your home-based electrical devices are plugged into a smart surge protector.** This is especially true for your entertainment center equipment. A power surge can damage these electronics very easily. Spend the money for a good quality smart surge protector and keep your equipment plugged into such a device. The smart surge protector can cut power to all devices on the strip once a control device is turned off to reduce phantom power drains. This can save you electricity consumption and significantly trim your power bill.

503. **Make use of a family plan package.** If multiple people in your family use one wireless plan, the price per line is often less than for a plan with a single line.

504. **Reduce your data plan.** As you are likely not going out as much because of the pandemic, you may be overpaying for data. You are likely using your home WiFi more for your data needs. Take stock of the amount of data you've used recently, then see whether you can find a plan to better suit your habits. If, on the other hand, you are a large user, ask to see if your provider has a shared data plan and include members of your family to save money.

505. **Select a slower speed for your Internet service.** Unless you're constantly streaming or playing high-definition video games, you probably won't notice the difference.

506. **Switch cell phone carriers to get a better deal.** For cell service, according to the US Bureau of Labor Statistics, an American household spent an average $1,118 in 2019. Switching carriers may save you money if the new provider cuts price breaks for new customers or if it offers lower price plans than your current carrier. You may also be able to get free access to a streaming service, such as Hulu, as an incentive to switch. Before changing, make sure the new provider that you're considering has strong coverage in your area.

507. **Cut back and/or bundle phone and Internet services.** Three necessities of modern life are phone, TV and Internet service. They can be bought separately or bundled, and the costs vary wildly. Figuring out the best deal takes effort since the monthly bills are full of numerously mandated charges. Be realistic and decide what you really need in data capacity and TV channels, then shop around for the best bundle or individual service.

508. **Eliminate your home phone service.** Only have a home phone if it is needed for a security or an educational reason. When was the last time you got an actual phone call that was not a telemarketer or a robocall? Just use your cell phone as your main contact number.

509. **Don't ignore Consumer Cellular for cell service.** Despite its annoying commercials of older Americans going on and on about what they have saved on their phone costs, there is potential value

for you here. Plans start at $20 per month, require no contract and include free activation and an extended risk-free guarantee.

510. **Don't upgrade your cell phone in a two-year cycle.** Do what quarterback Tom Brady has done—wait to upgrade. A lot of phone companies lock you into a two-year contract with a new phone. What this often ends up meaning is that at the end of the contract, you'll upgrade to a new phone. Even if you buy your phone outright instead of on a plan, for some reason, it's "accepted" that at the two-year mark it's time for a new phone. This isn't the case at all. The vast majority of cell phones will still work perfectly well after two years of use.

511. **Downgrade your cable plan in the summer months or if you are away for an extended period.** You can work with your cable company to reduce your plan. In the summer your household is likely to be more active and, hopefully, enjoying outdoor activities and vacation time together. You might save $100 doing this each year.

512. **If you need a new phone, buy one model older.** Unless you must have the newest technology, this idea can save you money. The phone will still have great function, work perfectly well and you'll be able to save hundreds of dollars in the process.

513. **Invest in a protective case or screen protector for your phone.** These purchases protect your phone from damage and help avoid costly repairs.

514. **Look to buy your telephone equipment and services from Amazon Wireless, AARP programs—Consumer Cellular, Net10.com or other large organizations.** Quite often these

organizations offer a lot of choices that are often cheaper than a store-bought phone.

515. **One way to save money on phone calls is to look for unlimited SMS plans offered by your operator.** This is particularly useful if you like to send a lot of text messages to your friends/family/business associates. Getting unlimited plans at discounted prices can surely be counted among the list of ways to save money on phone bills.

516. **Skip the router rental.** Your Internet provider might be charging you a monthly fee of about $15 for using their equipment, but you can buy your own modem and router and make up the cost in about a year.

517. **Consider voice over Internet protocol or VoIP telephone service.** This type of phone service has been very reliable from the reviews I have seen. Phone Power is a great option for Internet telephone service. It costs as little as $8.33 a month.

518. **Switch to a cheaper cell phone plan by shopping different providers or by changing your plan with your existing company.** I recently saved over 15% on my bill by reducing the number of minutes of usage and amount of data usage I needed. With the prevalence of WiFi hotspots and some discipline on your part, you can save money.

519. **Save money by replacing rather than repairing.** Today, with the high cost of at-home repair services and competitive prices for appliances, it is many times cheaper to replace rather than repair appliances.

TRANSPORTATION

520. **Buy your vehicle tires from Costco or other wholesale clubs.** Simply put, they cost a lot less than buying them at the dealer or even a chain tire store.

521. **Carpool to work if you still go to the office.** If you have an opportunity to share a ride with someone who does not have the virus, you can significantly reduce wear and tear on your car, save on gas and take advantage of carpooling lanes that might make it easier to get to work.

522. **Clean or replace your vehicle's air filter.** A clean air filter can improve your gas mileage by up to 11% according to CarsDirect. All you need to do is just follow the instructions in your vehicle's manual and you're good to go.

523. **Consider getting rid of your car.** Do you need a car? If there are alternatives that don't cost you too much time or money, it might be worth getting rid of your car altogether. For example, if you live in a major city, it might be easier and cheaper to take the subway, bus or walk. When you get rid of your car, you eliminate a lot of related expenses, e.g., car payments, insurance, repairs, registration, taxes, inspection, tickets, gasoline, etc.

524. **Cut back to one car in your household.** Trying to get by with one car may seem like a challenge, but it's well worth it if you are a two-car family. With the average car payment over $500 along with insurance, gas and maintenance, you can really do your budget a favor with just one car. The benefits do not include your contribution to an improved environment.

525. **Don't speed.** Not only is speeding inefficient in terms of gasoline usage, it also can get you pulled over and result in a high-priced traffic ticket. Tickets can cost you a bundle between a ticket and higher ongoing insurance premiums. It's far safer and more cost-efficient to just drive the speed limit.

526. **Drive conservatively to get the best gas mileage.** This would include not accelerating to red lights, stop signs or on the road when able. You should also consider driving at the speed limit and accelerating slowly to save gas.

527. **Drive your car longer**. With very high prices for new and newer model used cars, improvements in vehicle quality and the lower per mile cost for operating (including depreciation), it will likely pay you to hold on to your car for a few more years to avoid costly car payments. This is particularly the case if you have had a good repair history with your car. Drive it as long as it is cost effective to do so.

528. **Keep the tires on your automobiles properly inflated.** Once a month check the air pressure in your car tires by stopping by a local gas station that offers free air. If they aren't inflated to the optimal level, fill each one to the maximum recommended amount as stated in your manual. An investment in a $3 tire gauge may have a return on investment of more than 30 times its cost. A survey by Edmunds found that keeping your tires properly inflated could save the average driver $112 in gas money.

529. **Reduce the number of cars in your household.** The average American family owns 2.28 cars and more than a third of households own three or more vehicles. According to the Bureau of

Labor Statistics, the average household spends $10,742 a year on transportation, the second largest expense, with much of it for maintenance and gasoline. Living on one less car in the household can save big money. This is one of the tougher money saving tips because we love the freedom of movement our vehicles provide. It will take some getting used to but cutting back to just one car can save the average family nearly $5,000 a year.

530. **Rent out your least-used car.** Most cars are only used a few hours per week. Web services such as Turo, HyreCar or Getaround let you market a car that is otherwise just sitting around but charge you for it. They claim you can generate thousands of dollars a year.

531. **Stick to reliable, fuel-efficient cars.** Buying that sexy new model might not be the best long-term purchase you can make. A reliable and fuel-efficient car can save you thousands over the long haul. Let's say you drive a vehicle for 80,000 miles. If you choose a car that gets 25 miles per gallon over one that only gets 15, you'll save *2,133 gallons* of gas. At $3 a gallon, that's $6,399 in savings right there. Reliability can pay the same dividends.

532. **Use public transportation whenever possible.** Whether it's the subway, train, bus, cable car or ferry, you can beat expenses like gas, tolls and/or maybe even insurance by making your daily commute through public transportation. For a small percentage of the cost of owning a vehicle, you can get from one side of town to the next, to work and back and to important events. Each time you're able to leave the car behind, you'll be saving money.

533. **Use vehicle sharing options.** Instead of owning a car, you can use car-sharing services, slugging or carpooling when you need to.

534. **Carefully maintain your car.** That check engine light on your dashboard and that rattle in your muffler will cost a lot more tomorrow than it will today. Eliminate costly parts and labor charges rather than waiting until your car breaks down and it becomes an emergency situation, quite possibly requiring a loan. Effective maintenance includes keeping up with the service schedule, changing the oil as needed and keeping your tires properly inflated and rotated.

535. **Consider using the Carvana or CarMax Internet buying platforms for your next vehicle purchase.** There's no haggling involved, and your car may be delivered to your door. Plus, each company offers a seven-day, money-back guarantee. With the advent of the pandemic, your local vehicle dealers have also worked very hard to provide a seamless Internet buying experience.

536. **Consider fuel efficiency when you buy a new car.** This is especially true if you put a lot of miles on your vehicle or if you are in consistent stop-and-go traffic. As the new models roll out, purchasing an electric vehicle may be a wise choice.

537. **Consider switching to a less expensive car.** If you use your car regularly and can't get rid of it, it might be more practical to switch to a less expensive one.

538. **Consider walking more.** For example, walking a few blocks to the grocery store for that jug of milk will get you some exercise, ease off the environment and put off your next trip to the gas station. Every bit of activity helps keep you in shape.

539. **Do your own car maintenance.** Using YouTube as your teacher, you will find that you can do some minor car repairs, such as oil changes or brake pad replacement. Other fixes generally require a trained mechanic and could be costly. Be sure to understand your car's warranty and whether doing the repair yourself negates the coverage.

540. **Don't buy a new car as soon as you've paid off your car loan on the old one.** The advice is to wait as long as you practically can before committing to another car loan. A lot of people see paying off their car loan as an achievement—which it is! —that deserves a reward of a new, bigger car with a new, bigger loan. Instead, think about whether you really need a new car or if your existing one does the job perfectly well.

541. **Don't leave heavy objects in your vehicle.** Get rid of the heavy junk in your trunk; it's jacking up your gas mileage. The more a vehicle is carrying, the worse the gas mileage. An extra 100 pounds in the trunk cuts a typical car's fuel economy by 2% according to a November 2016 post on Autoblog. Dropping the weight can save nearly $40 a year.

542. **Drive a more affordable car.** Vehicle loan or lease payments can be very expensive. This debt service load stretches the cash budgets of many borrowers. In addition to the payment, you must also pay gas, maintenance, insurance, taxes, registration costs and more. You should look to buy a car that you can comfortably afford not what you can fit into your budget. The cash savings can be substantial.

543. **Fill your car up when you're down to a quarter tank of gas.** You won't be stuck going to the nearest, most expensive gas

station when your car is on empty. Use one of the gas savings apps like gasbuddy.com to find the lowest price for gas.

544. **Get gas at superstore centers.** Gas prices vary everywhere, but superstore centers tend to have the cheapest prices around when it comes to gas. Whether it's Costco or another superstore, these places tend to offer discounts if you already shop there. Since these stores often require you to buy in bulk, you'll be saving on groceries in addition to saving on gas.

545. **Get rewards for buying gasoline.** If your monthly gasoline expense feels like it's out of control, you can use a cash back credit card to get as much as 5% back when you fill up at the pump. You can also join one of the fuel rewards programs offered by the major gas station chains.

546. **Get your oil changed.** To avoid any major mishaps with your car, it's important to keep it in good shape. Get your oil changed based on the manufacturer's schedule so you can keep the warranty in place and save money by avoiding more costly mechanical issues.

547. **If you're selling your car, do it privately.** While it can be more hassle, selling a car privately can often get you thousands of dollars more compared to going through a dealer. This is true especially if your car is in above-average condition.

548. **Look for free parking.** Parking fees can really add up. Before heading to your destination, do some research and look for free parking spots. You may be able to find free parking using the parking app SpotAngels.

549. **Only use premium gas if your car requires it.** Unless your car needs the higher octane, you're just throwing away money. Higher octane doesn't give you more horsepower.

550. **Plan your day to save on transportation costs.** Does this sound familiar? You drive home from the grocery store and realize you've forgotten the dry cleaning. So, you drive to the dry cleaner, which is located two doors down from the grocery store. You return home and an hour later take your son to his music lesson in the same shopping center. Over time, those extra miles on your car can cost you a lot more in maintenance as well as gas expense. Keep lists for what you need to do, what you need to buy and where you need to go. It will not only save you money but a ton of time and frustration.

551. **Ride your bike when you can.** Many towns and cities are doing all they can to promote biking for commuting and running errands. If you live near your workplace or other places you frequent, consider investing in a bicycle. Riding even some of the time can save you serious cash on transportation, protect the environment and improve your health.

552. **Use cruise control.** Cruise control helps reduce wear and tear on your vehicle and can boost your fuel efficiency.

553. **Work to improve your gas mileage.** Start tracking your vehicle's gas mileage to determine the actual expense per gallon. Some simple tips include maintaining proper tire pressure, checking the tire alignment and losing that lead foot of yours by accelerating slowly.

TRAVEL

554. **Adopt cost-saving habits for travel.** If you want to get out of town for a vacation, there are plenty of money-saving tips. Some of the best ways to save money on your next vacation are: (1) Be flexible with your flight dates. A difference of just one day or two can sometimes save you over $100 per flight. (2) Travel in the mid or off season instead of the peak travel season. (3) Stay in an Airbnb. It is one of the best ways to save money while going on vacation. (4) Ask for a discount at your hotel. (5) Eat like a local. (6) Buy groceries for one meal per day and dine out less often.

555. **Carefully manage your vacation spending.** Instead of going on a long costly trip, pack up the car and see some of the sights in your area of the country. Look to take more three- or four-day breaks instead of a two-week break. Take advantage of our national park system and their surrounding areas for outdoor locations.

556. **Take that mandatory family trip to a Disney resort on a budget.** Regular tickets to Disney resorts are over $100 for ages 10 and up and seem to increase every year. There are ways to save, however, by bringing some of your own food and drink, eating outside the park and avoiding the gift shops. All of these actions will save you a significant amount. Disney World now allows outside food, and Disney cruises permit up to two bottles of wine or six beers in a carry-on. Although, the dining room corkage fee is $25.

557. **If possible, book your travel directly.** Booking directly with travel providers can yield savings and extra perks, such as free WiFi, fewer hidden fees and more flexibility.

558. **Bring your own food.** While the quality and variety of airport food offerings has greatly improved, they come with a high cost. To lower the cost of travel, bring/pack some of your own meals and snacks. This will save you money and likely be a healthier option.

559. **Look into booking boutique hotels.** Travelers looking for an alternative to a generic room in a large hotel chain property can opt for an inexpensive boutique hotel or bed and breakfast. There are numerous options across the country worth considering.

560. **Rent a vacation home for your family.** *One* way to accommodate family travel is to stay in short-term rental vacation homes offered by such services as Airbnb. Quite often, Airbnb vacation home rates are comparable or cheaper than a hotel, plus you usually have more room and that room may include a kitchen. Also, if you have several members of your family vacationing with you, you can split the cost of a house, which is cheaper than it would be for individual hotel room reservations.

561. **Save money on souvenirs.** When taking a trip or traveling to a foreign country, look for souvenirs that are small, lightweight and of good quality. You will thank me for this suggestion when you downsize in your later years. Focus on buying stuff you can eat or small reminders that can easily fit on a shelf or desk.

562. **Avoid booking vacations during busy holidays and travel days.** This is a simple idea, but it's an easy way to save. Usually flying Monday through Thursday is cheaper than flying over a weekend. Wednesdays are the often the cheapest days for travel. Plan your trip from Wednesday to Wednesday to get the lowest fare.

563. **Avoid paying foreign transaction fees.** Get a credit card that does not charge extra for foreign transactions. This can save you a lot if you travel to foreign locations or when making purchases in a foreign currency while at home.

564. **Book your trips using unused time-shares.** Change happens to time-share owners who can't use their booked weeks. There are websites like Trading Places International or RedWeek where you can book these accommodations at steep discounts.

565. **Book your flights to travel on a holiday.** You can normally get additional savings by actually flying on a holiday. If you have the time and don't mind this, you can save money by flying on Thanksgiving day or Christmas day. I did this during the week between Christmas and the New Year when my children were older.

566. **Book your hotel just out of town or away from the major tourist area.** Hotels are often cheaper and more tranquil when located farther from the city center or from major attractions. You may find that the major attractions are a 10-minute subway or taxi ride away and you can save accommodation dollars.

567. **Check your credit card for additional benefits.** Some cards offer surprising rewards, like travel insurance, access to airline clubs/lounges, credits for TSA PreCheck, luggage fee reimbursement, roadside assistance, free museum entry and complimentary subscriptions to premium offerings from Lyft and DoorDash.

568. **Don't pay baggage fees.** Almost every airline charges for luggage. You can avoid these fees if you have an airline-affiliated credit card or by carrying your luggage on the plane. Watch-out for budget airlines such as Allegiant, Frontier and Spirit, which collect fees even for carry-ons.

569. **Never fly when you can drive.** This is one idea that the pandemic has highlighted. Air travel has become so common that many people use it as a default choice whenever they travel. If you are traveling with family, plan to drive instead of flying, especially if the trip is within a few hundred miles. By driving, not only do you save the expense of buying airline tickets for each family member, but you also have a car when you arrive at your destination. If your family car is not up to the task, you can rent a compact car for $300-$400 per week, which is roughly the cost of a single airline ticket to many destinations. In this pandemic-impacted world, traveling by car can help reduce possible exposure to people with the virus.

570. **Plan early or book late.** Planning early comes with many perks, such as being the first to book at the lowest cost. As soon as you get your family's schedule for the upcoming year, plan vacations around days off. When my kids were young, I tried to book our vacations on non-holiday days off from school, such as teacher in-service days, to avoid spiked rates. On the flipside, though,

there are numerous websites that offer discounted travel arrangements for the last-minute traveler.

571. **Research multiple sites for low airfares.** Want to plan your dream vacation and save money doing it? Don't rely on a single airline search engine to show you all inexpensive fares. Some discount carriers do not allow their flights to be listed in these third-party searches. You need to check their websites separately.

572. **Steer clear of hotel minibars.** This tip will save inexperienced travelers the unexpected surprise of minibar charges. It's not as simple as refraining from eating or drinking anything. Some hotel minibars have a built-in sensor that may be triggered by merely moving the items. Look over the bill before checking out to make sure there aren't any accidental charges. I have done this for years and saved by not paying charges that were not mine but related to the prior room guest.

573. **Substantially reduce your travel costs by paying for travel costs using credit card reward points.** One of my favorite money-saving tips is to get reward points on as many of my purchases as I can. I have set this up such that in most years I qualify for 15 free hotel nights each year. This saves me on average about $6,000 per year. To make this one of the best ways to save money, you will need to pay your credit card bill in full each month and stay up to date on how best to accumulate and use points.

574. **Take a staycation.** A staycation is when you take a vacation by exploring the city you live in. This is one of the best ways to save money because it still involves leisure time. By taking a staycation, you will save money on airfare or other means of

transportation, likely spare yourself any unnecessary exposure to the virus and you can even take it while sleeping in the comfort of your own home. The idea of a staycation is to explore your area as a tourist would. You could make a list of all of the places in your area that you've been meaning to explore, from parks, museums, restaurants, etc. I'm sure there are tons of things to do and places to visit that you have never had the chance to see before! This can be a great way to treat yourself. You'll pretty much be on vacation, but you'll save the expense of a typical get-away vacation.

575. **Take volunteer vacations for a way to see the world and also give back.** The experience can be personally rewarding and much less expensive than a resort.

576. **Use Skype and WhatsApp when you travel.** Traveling internationally can result in hefty phone and international roaming charges. When communicating from most major locations worldwide, you should be able to find a free app to use over WiFi to communicate for free.

WATER

577. **Drink less bottled water.** Bottled water is substantially more than the cost of the same amount of tap water. According to the website the waterproject.org, the average American spends about $100 a year on bottled water. Consider switching to a filter, and let it pay for itself.

578. **Install a low-flow toilet to reduce water usage.** If you need to replace a toilet, consider going to a low-flow model. If you don't

have a low-flow model, installing one can save you a great deal in water usage. If you don't need a new toilet, you can reduce the amount of water you use per flush by placing a plastic bottle full of water and weighted with pebbles in your water tank.

579. **Fix your leaking pipes.** It can save a vast amount of water and cost.

580. **Install shower heads that control the amount of water flow.**

581. **Take shorter showers.**

582. **Take showers instead of baths.**

583. **Use less water when you're brushing your teeth, shampooing or shaving.**

584. **Use pasta water for watering household plants.**

WEDDINGS

585. **Pick a less-crowded date to wed.** If there's more demand for a given date, you'll usually pay a higher price for a venue. You will likely get a discount for choosing a less popular month, such as January or February, or a weekday for your nuptials.

586. **Choose a location for your ceremony that can also accommodate the reception.** I was married in a community center specifically designed for cultural and social events. Picking a spot that doesn't usually cater to weddings can help you save money and give your nuptials a special, unique feel. One proviso is to make sure the location is equipped to handle a large event. Don't forget

to factor in rental fees for items such as tents, lighting or furniture that you will need.

587. **Consider a late morning ceremony followed by a luncheon reception.** Scheduling the event earlier in the day can save you the expense of booking the venue for the entire day. Ask the venue if they would be willing to split the expense and the day by offering the evening hours to another bridal party.

588. **Save on invitations by going digital or printing your own.** You can send electronic invitations for free with Joy, a wedding website that also lets you manage your guest list and track RSVPs. With today's home printers, wedding invitations are easy to do yourself. Tap a design-savvy friend or buy a downloadable template on a site such as Etsy. Then print the invitations at home or at your neighborhood Staples or another store. Either way, you'll save a couple hundred dollars versus going with a professionally printed invitation.

589. **Look for alternatives to save money on the wedding dress.** Check out discount department stores, bridal consignment locations, vintage clothing stores or the dress that a family member wore. There are a number of sources to find a beautiful dress while saving money for other needs.

590. **Get creative with your choice of flowers.** Make your own centerpieces by using flowers grown locally, seasonally available flowers and with decorations from your favorite craft stores. This can add a personal decorative touch to your affair. We were able to save on flowers by moving certain arrangements from the room in which our ceremony was held into the reception area.

591. **Make wise food and beverage decisions.** Meet with a few caterers to compare and sample food options. Purchasing the wedding cake through your caterer can also save on the overall expense.

592. **You don't need the most artistic cake creation.** Save money by selecting a less grandiose decorated cake or serve a non-traditional dessert like your favorite cupcakes or cookies.

593. **Be selective with your guest list.** Do you really need to invite that old friend from second grade that you haven't seen in 20-some years? Some of the best wedding planners advise you to keep the guest list small. This will help save on all aspects of your wedding. Share this special day with those dear family members and close friends that enrich your life.

594. **Limit your desire to create a full-length feature film of your wedding day.** What can I say about this subject in this era of Instagram and smartphones? Carefully think about what you want to memorialize in photos and on video. It will save you money on photographer and videographer fees and costs.

ZOOM TOWN MOVING COSTS

With the advent of remote working, many people now have the opportunity to live wherever they want. This has people moving to new locations. This section gives you some ideas on how to save expenses on your Zoom Town move.

595. **Understand your new location.** Be sure you understand all of the costs of living in your new Zoom Town. Research the cost of living, tax laws, housing market, school systems and local

economic conditions. This research will pay you dividends as you settle into your new living arrangements and avoid any major negative surprises.

596. **Find as many free boxes as possible before moving.** You will discover that moving boxes are expensive and that you will need more than you think to get your possessions packed. Before you start packing, seek out free moving supplies from various stores, online marketplaces, community groups and friends. This is a great way to save hundreds of dollars on moving expenses. You can find potential moving boxes on Craigslist, Freecycle, U-Haul Box Exchange, Nextdoor and local Facebook groups.

597. **Choose a cheaper date and time to move.** One of the easiest ways to save money during a move is to simply choose the right moving date. When hiring a professional moving company, you can save money by being flexible with your move date. First, avoid moving during the "peak moving season" from May to August. Instead, opt for a mid-week, mid-month moving date between the months of September and April. Second, ask the company when the best time for them would be. You may find that the moving company has a partial shipment headed for your new location that you could benefit from.

598. **Get quotes from at least three movers.** Each mover's estimate will require an in-person inspection, phone interview or a video survey of your belongings before giving you a quote. If you're moving out of state or a long distance, the move cost will be determined by the weight of your items. To obtain the most accurate quote, be sure to tell the person quoting the estimate which items you will be moving on your own. Always check out the Internet

reviews for each company to ensure you are hiring a reputable mover.

599. **De-clutter before packing.** Whether you're downsizing or simply looking to de-clutter, getting rid of your unused items is one of the easiest ways to cut costs during a move. By eliminating worn clothing, out-of-date electronics and unnecessary furniture, your move will weigh less—making the relocation less expensive. There is nothing worse than paying to move items you throw away or donate upon your arrival in your new location.

600. **Carefully review your moving contract.** Be sure you understand how you will be charged for the move, the cost of replacement insurance coverage, packing costs and financial limitations on the moving company's liability. Taking the time to perform an in-depth review of your contract can save money, time and misunderstandings on billing matters.

CHAPTER 3

FINAL THOUGHTS - LOOKING FOR COST SAVINGS

According to the Bureau of Labor Statistics, the typical American household spent just over $63,000 in 2019 for the goods and services needed to support their family members. At the same time, the majority of household budgets were as stretched as they could be to fund these expenses. In this book I have tried to provide 600 cost-saving ideas for you to consider and possibly use. To really focus on consistently saving money, you need to make cost savings one of your good money habits.

It is often stated that humans are creatures of habit. Our habits control more of our lives than we realize. They are things we do unconsciously. For instance, you might enjoy having two scrambled eggs and toast in the morning before you begin your day. If, for some reason, you don't have them, you are likely to feel as if some part of your day is incomplete.

Making changes to your cash budget and expenses and learning how to save your money takes time. You can't expect to move from your current financial behavior to good money actions overnight. However, the more you practice your new money habits, the sooner they will settle into your mind as normal behavior.

Studies show that it takes around 90 days to break and change our habits. Therefore, if you give up your eggs and toast in the morning, you'll only feel strange about it for a few weeks. After a while, you'll stop thinking about it and life will move on.

Lastly, don't think of saving money as being cheap. You are simply making better use of one of your most precious resources—cash. Every household needs to learn how to be more frugal with their expenses. In times of pandemic-influenced economic uncertainty, learning how to live with less, while still enjoying life, is an exercise worth practicing.

ABOUT THE AUTHOR

Harry N. Stout is the author of the FinancialVerse personal finance books and a former financial services executive with over 30 years' experience in all aspects of personal finance. A certified public accountant by training, he has worked in countries worldwide helping consumers save, financially protect their families and prepare for the later years of their lives. He has been the President and/or Chief Executive Officer of several large US life insurance, annuity and advice businesses. He has written for numerous financial publications, hosted national podcasts and been seen on national television. He is acknowledged as a thought leader on personal financial management, retirement planning, investments and life insurance. Harry is a graduate of Drexel University in Philadelphia, Pennsylvania.